Ralph R. Leutenegger
University of Wisconsin—Milwaukee

THE SOUNDS OF AMERICAN ENGLISH

AN INTRODUCTION TO PHONETICS

SCOTT, FORESMAN AND COMPANY

To Louise, Renee, Craig, Michelle, Curt, and Scott

FOREWORD

Much of what might ordinarily go into a Foreword has already gone into Professor Leutenegger's Preface, with the aims of which the present writer heartily concurs. All too often the teaching of phonetics becomes little more than a stylized code for transcribing the letters of conventional spelling into a standardized system of phonetic letters, with little or no awareness of the acoustic values involved. Thirty years ago many American students, under the supposition that they were learning to use "Standard English," were induced to write phonetic transcriptions which supposedly represented a style of speech which teachers and students alike thought representative of a style of speech used by some Londoners. Though this unrealistic approach to phonetics has subsided, other unrealistic approaches remain, chiefly based on a particular teacher's notion of correctness which may be no more than a rationalization of that teacher's own speech habits.

The important thing for the student is to analyze what he actually hears, first in his own speech, later in that of others. Analysis must precede evaluation. The concept of correctness is essentially one of conformity, and no intelligent concept of correctness can be achieved before the student has become vividly aware of the nature and extent of the conformity which people accept. Short of this, the results of "self-improvement" are quite as likely to be laughable as laudable. Moreover, without such an awareness of what people actually say, the student can never develop an awareness of the great possibilities the English language offers him, or show proper respect for the language.

Professor Leutenegger has provided a fresh and uniquely motivated approach to this quest. The conscientious student should profit from it.

C. K. THOMAS,

Professor of Speech,
University of Florida

TABLE OF CONTENTS

PREFACE

WHY STUDY PHONETICS?

Frequently college students majoring in speech are heard to say: "But why must *I* study phonetics? That's strictly for speech correctionists." Unfortunately this attitude prevents many students from realizing full value from the course.

When this attitude is encountered, one looks for a reason. Is the student lazy? Is the teaching material uninteresting? What is the attitude of the speech department toward this basic tool? Frequently the answer to a specific student's problem is a combination of many factors. Unfortunately, the negative attitude is due many times to the student's failure to understand the need to master what appears to be an esoteric skill.

The author believes that phonetic training is basic to improving your own speech, as well as to helping others improve theirs. Certainly, remedial speech teachers can more quickly recognize and more precisely record articulation errors as a result of such training. Phonetic training is also necessary for both actors and directors working with stage dialects, and it is an indispensable tool for objective study or research in linguistics. It is the writer's conviction that the improvement of our articulation and pronunciation depends on our mental awareness of the speech sounds we utter. The most efficient way to heighten this awareness, or *auditory self-perception,* is through phonetic training. Thus, the author regards as a truism the viewpoint of George Sampson, who believes that "a teacher of speech untrained in phonetics is as useless as a doctor untrained in anatomy." (Kenyon, 1950, p. iii.)

The primary aim of this book is to train you, the student, to hear the sounds of American speech—particularly those you yourself utter—and to transcribe these sounds by means of phonetic symbols. Two secondary aims are to give you an understanding of how American speech sounds are produced and to provide you with an elementary knowledge of phoneticians' terminology and areas of study.

BEGIN LEARNING NOW

The author of this book enjoys teaching phonetics, and he is convinced that phonetics can be fun for most students. This is not just a professor's wishful thinking, but is the result of observing students' reactions to the subject for more than a decade. The conviction rests on one condition: the student must be willing to do the necessary groundwork at the *beginning* of the course. Phonetics is a cumulative skill like geometry; if the subject is ignored during the first few weeks, it will require an overwhelming amount of work to catch up.

Students have frequently admitted, "If only I had forced myself to study at the beginning of the course, I know I could have done much better." At first, when your choice of symbols for transcription is limited to one out of three or four, there is little confusion, and phonetics may seem deceptively easy. Trouble is likely to arise, however, when the choice becomes one out of twelve or more vowel sounds. Conscientiously completing the drills and exercises in this book should help make phonetic transcription a relatively easy accomplishment. But you must concentrate fully on the task.

One cannot master this skill by routinely recording pencil squiggles on paper while daydreaming. If your mind is not focused on your work, you are probably learning little if anything. Stop studying until you can bring your mind back to the sound symbols you are learning. This may sound like strange advice to appear in the preface to a book. It is here because past students have said, "This is important to know *at the beginning*."

A NOTE TO TEACHERS

The author has long observed speech students who say they have "learned" the phonetic alphabet. A sterile type of intellectualization of the phonetic symbols sometimes occurs, particularly when students "learn" phonetics in a one- or two-week period. Most students quickly learn to write the proper phonetic symbol for a given isolated sound and can learn to transcribe individual words as they think they pronounce them. Too often, however, many of these same students are unable to detect pronunciations that differ from their own and are unaware of the subtle sound modifications in their own speech when they move from single sounds to isolated words to words in context. Nor do their ears detect such changes in the speech of others.

To a great extent, training the ear is a matter of self-teaching, and the systematic progression of exercises in this book is planned to aid the student in self-instruction. The contents of the book should be augmented by verbal dictation in the classroom, so that each student has the opportunity to hear and transcribe speech sounds and to have his transcription checked. It is hoped that the combination of visual and auditory drills will bring the student to a genuine awareness of the sounds of speech, as a necessary basis for self-improvement in articulation and pronunciation.

The problem of what to include or exclude in a book is always a difficult one, and obviously the present text cannot cover thoroughly all aspects of phonetics. Thus it was decided to include a greatly abridged discussion of respiration, phonation, and resonation in Appendix A, on the grounds that a detailed treatment of these subjects was beyond the scope of this book. This skeletal outline should be augmented by the instructor, by additional readings, or by course prerequisites.

Occasionally a technical word or phrase is used in the text in such a way that it is not convenient to discuss its meaning. In such cases, a definition will be given in the Glossarial Index (Appendix C). Students should be urged to familiarize themselves with this Index, referred to throughout this book as the *G.I.*

Every effort has been made to discuss each sound and to give its phonetic symbol before requiring students to use it in transcription exercises. The only exceptions are (1) in the exercises in Chapter 1, and (2) in the chapter summaries. Since the summaries use only terminology already presented, the student should not find the phonetic transcription difficult to read.

Since the Kenyon and Knott *Pronouncing Dictionary of American English* is the chief phonetic pronunciation reference in America, the present book usually follows its transcriptions. Systematic adherence to its transcription, however, does not indicate the author's complete agreement with its style but rather represents an arbitrary solution for the convenience of those who prefer to rely on the dictionary for transcription confirmation.

Reliance on this dictionary has stylized the transcriptions used in the crossword puzzles, particularly in the matter of final -*y* endings and in words containing the post-vocalic [r]. For some words the author finds these transcriptions open to alternatives. For instance, although pronunciation of the word-ending -*y* varies in words such as *pity* and *daily*, Kenyon and Knott give only the [ɪ] ending. Despite such minor reservations, the Kenyon and Knott *Pronouncing Dictionary* is a milestone in phonetic scholarship, and students will do well to keep the book handy at all times.

ACKNOWLEDGMENTS

The author wishes to acknowledge the help of the many people who have contributed directly and indirectly to the development of this book. While the book has benefited greatly from their help, none of them can be held in any way responsible for any of the omissions, inaccuracies, or obscurities which might have persisted into the final printed copy.

To Dr. Douglas Ehninger, for his initial confidence in the projected manuscript, the author expresses his heartfelt appreciation. He is grateful to Dr. Stanley H. Ainsworth for his encouragement during the book's early stages and to Dr. Hilda B. Fisher for her detailed criticism of one of the first drafts. The full extent of the author's indebtedness to Dr. James F. Curtis — both as his former teacher and as a critic of this manuscript — would be difficult to measure and to acknowledge fairly. His guidance has been invaluable. The influence of Professor C. K. Thomas' scholarship permeates most of this book. His close reading and penetrating criticism of the last two drafts have added immeasurably to the soundness of this text. For his extensive counsel and continuing encouragement, as well as for his generous offer to write a foreword to this book, the author is extremely grateful.

For her assistance in typing the manuscript, the author wishes to thank Mrs. Christine McCarthy. In addition, he is indebted to Lowell Hammer for checking the final versions of each of the crossword puzzles and to the author's many phonetics students, some of whom were working the phonetic crossword puzzles as early as 1953. Finally he wishes to acknowledge his gratitude to the various teachers who have inspired him and to the many phoneticians whose field work is the source for most of the content of this book.

chapter 1

AN INTRODUCTION

TO THE SOUNDS OF OUR SPEECH

Phonetics, phonemes, allophones
The phonetic alphabet
Pronunciation standards
Word divisions
Beginning drills and exercises
Study suggestions

Phonetics, Phonemes, Allophones

The term *phonetics* may be defined as "the science of speech sounds," or as the scientific study of speech sounds from the standpoints of their production, reception, and symbolization. *Phonetics* is also used to designate the symbols used to represent speech sounds visually. Thus, we say that he wrote his name in phonetics; for example, Ralph is written [rælf] in phonetics. Often a distinction is made between experimental and applied phonetics. *Experimental phonetics* is "a laboratory science concerned with measurement, description, and analysis of speech signals, their production, and the processes by which they are perceived and interpreted" (Travis, 1957, p. 55).[1] *Applied phonetics*, on the other hand, is a practical discipline; it relates the knowledge gained from experimental phonetics to the understanding and speaking of languages. It draws also on *linguistics* – the science of language, or of languages – which includes *morphology* (see G.I.[2]), and *semantics* (see G.I.) as well as all aspects of phonetics. It is with the field of applied phonetics that this book is chiefly concerned.

Most elementary courses in phonetics deal primarily with the symbolizing of distinctions among *phonemes*. A *phoneme* can be defined as a family of sounds none of which is distinctively different from the others. Let us see if we can

---

1. For full information on the references cited in this text, see the Bibliography, pages 163-164.

2. The abbreviation *G.I.* refers to the Glossarial Index, pages 165-168.

understand what is meant by this definition. Obviously "a family of sounds" means several or a group of sounds. What, however, is meant by "distinctively different"? Say aloud slowly the words *cool, cot,* and *keep.* Listen carefully to the *k* sound in each. You will note that each of the three *k* sounds is slightly different. None, however, is so unlike the others that we interpret it as a sound other than *k.* For example, we don't hear *tool,* no matter how unlike the *k* sound in *cool* is to the first sound in *cot* or in *keep.* These three *k* sounds are *not* distinctively different. They are therefore considered members of the same sound family, or phoneme, and are represented by the same phonemic symbol.

By listening very closely, we may perceive extremely slight differences between sounds which we have always presumed to be the same. These differences between sounds are usually more easily detected when we concentrate on vowel rather than consonant sounds. If we listen to the way different people pronounce the word *pin,* we hear different sounds between the two consonants. Sometimes the sound is so different from the normal one that we say the speaker has mispronounced the word as *pen.* In this case, the vowel sound is distinctively different from the sound (or family of sounds) that most people associate with a correctly pronounced *pin.* it belongs to another phoneme.

Although a phoneme may include slightly varying sounds (hence its description as a family of sounds), each phoneme is a *distinctive* sound unit: it is different enough from other phonemes to be useful in distinguishing meaning. If, for example, the vowel sound in *get* is distorted enough in a certain direction, the listener will hear the word as *gate.* The two words are differentiated by different vowel phonemes.

The individual, *nondistinctive* sounds which comprise a phoneme (or sound family) are called *allophones* of that phoneme. For example, the three different *k* sounds in *cool, cot,* and *keep* are allophones of the [k] phoneme. The chief reason for these very slight differences in sound is the effect of preceding and/or following sounds upon any sound's production. All neighboring sounds influence the way a given sound is produced. The slight differences in the manner of production give rise to the slightly different acoustic end results which we label *allophones.*

We frequently hear the word *phonetics* used in adjective form. When we speak of a phonetic language, we mean one that uses an alphabet which approaches the phonetic principle of "one sound – one symbol." The languages most closely approaching this principle are modern Turkish, Finnish, and Czech, and, to a lesser degree, Spanish and Italian. In this sense, we might ask ourselves if English is a phonetic language. One way to answer this question is to compare aloud the words in the following five word groups:

1. cent   can't   cello
2. physics   fix
3. vow   plough   our   hour   sauerkraut
4. conscious   fiction   Chicago   glacier   anxious
   pressure   shade   schottische   sure   tension
5. people   meat   meet   Phoenix   relief   receive
   ego   Aegis   key   police

Another answer could be arrived at by sounding out hundreds of words which *are* phonetic in their spelling. For example: *ad-lib, bland, club, drab, end, fry, gold, hunt, invent, jolt.* Is English a phonetic language? What do you think?

The Phonetic Alphabet

The wide divergence between the sounds and the spelling of our language has caused innumerable problems and called attention to the need for a system of symbols by which the sounds of our language and others could be recorded. At one time or another you have probably complained about the inadequacy or confusion of the diacritical marks (see G.I.) used by dictionaries to indicate pronunciation.

In 1886 a group of language teachers in France formed the International Phonetic Association, which in 1888 published the first version of the International Phonetic Alphabet (IPA).[3] In the strictest sense, this is not a truly international alphabet, since it is based on the Latin alphabet. However, the IPA appears to have international usefulness for phoneticians and has been used with a number of non-Latin languages.

The IPA was designed "primarily to meet practical linguistic needs, such as putting on record the phonetic or phonemic structure of languages, furnishing learners of foreign languages with phonetic transcriptions to assist them in acquiring the pronunciation, and working out Romanic orthographies (see G.I.) for languages written in other systems or for languages hitherto unwritten" (*The Principles of the International Phonetic Association*, 1949, p. 1). In terms of contemporary speech education, it is apparent that an actor trained in phonetics can more readily master dialects for stage, radio, or television performance. Remedial speech teachers can learn to recognize articulation errors more quickly and to record them more precisely. Indeed, any individual seeking to improve his own speech can grasp correct pronunciations more precisely by utilizing the phonetic alphabet and dictionary.

The symbols used in this book are based on the alphabet of the International Phonetic Association, with some additions used by many American phoneticians today. These symbols appear in the following chart and inside the front cover of this book.

Pronunciation Standards

Teachers of speech are continually called upon to determine "What is *the* correct pronunciation?" Actually, there is no one socially preferred standard of pronunciation in the United States as there still is in England. The best reference an individual can use in determining the standard for *him* is the speech of the educated members of his own community. This type of reference obviously demands keen listening.

---

3. Some attempts to set up a phonetic system were made even earlier, notably Henry Sweet's Broad Romic system, published in 1877. For a detailed account of this and other precursors of the IPA, see Albright, 1958, pages 1-46.

PHONETIC SYMBOLS USED IN THIS TEXT[4]

Page	Phonetic Symbol	Key Words	Additional Spellings of Sound
24	[p]	part	rope, stopped, hiccough
25	[b]	be	rubbed, cupboard
26	[t]	to	butt, debt, raked, indict, yacht, Thomas, receipt, might
27	[d]	do	add, rubbed, could
28	[k]	keep	cue, sick, account, lake, ache, walk, khaki
28	[g]	give	egg, ghost, guest
31	[f]	fame	off, phrase, laugh
31	[v]	vest	of, have, Stephen
70	[θ]	thin	
70	[ð]	the	
32	[s]	see	miss, scent, schism, cinder, psalm, sword, waltz
32	[z]	zoo	fuzz, raise, scissors, xylophone
72	[ʃ]	ship	issue, sugar, pension, gracious, ration, champagne, anxious, schottische, conscious
72	[ʒ]	lesion	leisure, azure, negligee
34	[h]	he	whole
30	[m]	milk	summer, comb
65	[m̩]	chasm	
30	[n]	no	inn, pneumonia, Wednesday, mnemonic, knife, gnash
65	[n̩]	sadden	botany
33	[l]	lake	tell
65	[l̩]	saddle	
34	[w]	wig	language
76	[hw] or [ʍ]	whig	
35	[r]	red	merry, rhetoric, wrist
77	[j]	yes	onion
74	[tʃ]	chew	cello, witch, feature

---

4. This table does not include nondistinctive diphthongs (pages 00, 00, 000, 000) or centering diphthongs (pages 000,000).

Page	Phonetic Symbol	Key Words	Additional Spellings of Sound
74	[dʒ]	*just*	ra*ge*, *g*em, dod*ge*, sol*d*ier
67	[ŋ]	si*ng*	a*n*chor, ha*n*dkerchief, to*ngue*
39	[i]	*see*	*ea*t, p*eo*ple, ch*ie*f, perc*ei*ve, b*e*, k*ey*, ph*oe*nix, rav*i*ne, C*ae*sar
42	[ɪ]	*si*t	h*e*re, h*ea*r, s*ie*ve, h*y*mn, bus*i*ness, wom*e*n, gu*i*ld
47	[e]	*a*che	*ai*m, b*ei*ge, gr*ea*t, pl*ay*, gr*ey*, g*au*ge
51	[ɛ]	*e*nd	s*ai*d, p*ea*r, s*ay*s, h*ei*r, l*eo*pard, fr*ie*nd, *a*ny
54	[æ]	*ca*n't	l*au*gh, h*a*lf
57	[a][5]	*ca*n't	l*au*gh, h*a*lf
61	[ɝ]	*ear*n	w*or*st, f*ir*, f*ur*, p*urr*, g*er*m, m*yr*tle, j*our*ney, col*o*nel
61	[ɜ][5]	*ear*n	w*or*st, f*ir*, f*ur*, p*urr*, g*er*m, m*yr*tle, j*our*ney, col*o*nel
61	[ɚ]	ladd*er*	s*ur*prise, sail*or*, li*ar*
59	[ʌ]	*up*	s*o*n, t*ou*gh, g*u*ll, d*oe*s, bl*oo*d
59	[ə]	*sofa*	s*u*cceed, fam*ou*s, barg*ai*n, speci*me*n, kingd*o*m, N*o*ah
80	[u]	*foo*d	r*u*de, wh*o*se, thr*ou*gh, thr*ew*, sh*oe*s, gr*ou*p, bl*ue*
82	[ʊ]	*boo*k	c*ou*ld, f*u*lly, w*o*lf
86	[o]	r*o*pe	*oa*k, th*ou*gh, s*ow*n, s*ew*, g*oe*s, y*eo*men, sh*ou*lder, b*eau*
88	[ɔ]	*au*ght	r*aw*, c*ou*gh, abr*oa*d, g*o*ne, fl*oo*r, th*ou*ght, *a*ll
89	[ɑ]	f*ar*m	h*o*t, h*o*nest
91	[ɒ][5]	f*o*rest	w*a*nt, h*o*nest, l*au*ndry
96	[aɪ]	sk*y*	wr*i*te, h*eigh*t, *ai*sle, b*uy*, l*ye*, *eye*, *aye*, p*ie*, s*igh*
99	[aʊ]	*ou*t	b*ou*gh, cr*ow*d, h*our*, s*au*erkraut
101	[ɔɪ]	b*oy*	br*oi*l

---

5. These sounds are most frequently heard in sections of the East and South.

Your ears are your best guides in determining your own pronunciation standards, but you can also consult reputable dictionaries and books dealing with speech standards — making sure to use the newest editions, since pronunciation standards change with the passage of time. The Bibliography lists several of these sources.

Standards of good speech include the minute differences in the speech of educated persons in both formal and informal situations. Formal speech generally includes public speeches by national and community leaders, the preaching of the clergy, and the speeches of well-educated persons speaking in any formal situation.

How does this formal speech differ from the informal or more colloquial (see G.I.) speech of the same people? In the formal situation they tend to speak more slowly, they produce the individual sounds more painstakingly and clearly, they give some of the subordinate words in the sentence an emphasis closely approaching that of the main words, they avoid contractions, they pause longer between thoughts, they use greater variety in pitch (see G.I.) and loudness. Many of these differences can be attributed to the difficulty of making your voice heard and understood under less than optimum acoustic conditions. Perhaps keeping your speech "audience-oriented" is the best criterion in determining your speech standards for any particular occasion.

Various factors tend to stabilize American speech and pronunciation standards from community to community. These factors include the influence of the school systems, the mobility of today's population, books (particularly dictionaries), magazines, newspapers, radio, television, and motion pictures. The stabilizing influence of many of these factors, however, has been a matter of the recent past. In our early history the American colonies were relatively isolated from each other and reflected different speech origins, since the colonists came from different dialect regions of the British Isles. Successive migrations from other European countries and the waves of western movement in the United States all had their highly complex influences on spoken English in America. Readers wishing to study the development of regional patterns of speech will find several informative books listed in the Bibliography.

In the early part of this century, students of American pronunciation delineated three major speech regions: (1) *Eastern* (comprising New York City and its environs plus the New England states east of the Connecticut River); (2) *Southern* (all the states of the Confederacy — that is, Virginia, North Carolina, South Carolina, Tennessee, Georgia, Florida, Alabama, Mississippi, Arkansas, Louisiana, and Texas — plus sections of Maryland, West Virginia, Kentucky, and Oklahoma); and (3) *General American* (the remainder of the country).

In the past quarter century, evidence has accumulated which demonstrates that this dialect (see G.I.) division is grossly oversimplified. Linguistic geographers (see G.I.), such as C. K. Thomas and Hans Kurath, are plotting increasing numbers of major U.S. dialect areas (ten in the 1958 edition of Thomas' *Phonetics of American English*).

The dialect differences presented in this book will be chiefly gross differences corresponding roughly to the three original dialect areas. Detailed dialectal distinctions are not within the scope and intention of this book. The bulk of the transcriptions given here are most typical of that part of the section formerly labeled *General American*, which Thomas (1958, pp. 229-231) calls *North Central.* (See Figure 1.) The teacher using this book presumably will aid the student in clarifying the dialect considered standard for his section of the country.

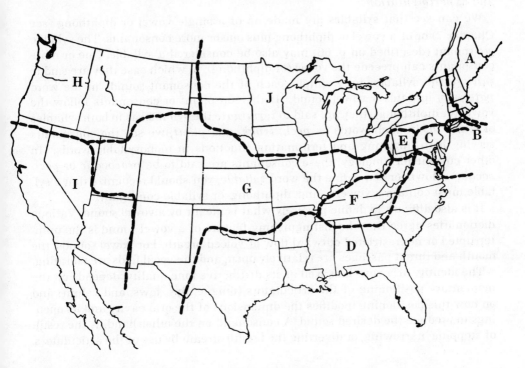

Fig. 1. Map showing the major regional speech areas. A: Eastern New England; B: New York City; C: Middle Atlantic; D: Southern; E: Western Pennsylvania; F: Southern Mountain; G: Central Midland; H: Northwest; I: Southwest; J: North Central.[6]

Word Divisions

From our experience in reading, writing, and spelling, we have come to regard the word as the basic unit of our language. Our study of phonetics will begin, therefore, with individual words and proceed to the consideration of speech as a process.

Some of us learned words as totalities; others learned them as meaningful groups of syllables. We will start on the latter basis, recognizing that words con-

6. From Charles K. Thomas, *An Introduction to the Phonetics of American English,* 2nd ed., page 232. New York: The Ronald Press Company, 1958.

sist of various parts called syllables. Attempts to define the syllable have met with varying degrees of success.[7] Many dictionary definitions describe the syllable as a part of a word uttered on an uninterrupted impulse of the voice. All of the words in the sentence "He is a dunce" are *monosyllabic*; each word contains one syllable, or a single vocal impulse. *Polysyllabic* words are those which contain more than one syllable, such as *fishing, referee, paternity, geometrical,* and *experimentation.*

We can see that syllables are made up of a single vowel or diphthong (see Chapter 7) or of a vowel or diphthong plus one or more consonants. The syllabic consonant (described on p. 66) may also be considered a syllable. One or more consonants can precede the vowel (or diphthong), in which case they are said to *initiate* the syllable; for example, each of the consonant sounds in the word *paternity* initiates a vowel sound.[8] If the consonant or consonants follow the vowel (or diphthong), they are said to *terminate* the syllable, as in both syllables of *unearth.* In such words as *peck, truck,* and *plant,* we see the consonants serving both initiating and terminating functions in monosyllabic words. (In other current terminology, these consonants are said to be *prevocalic* or *postvocalic.*) However you define the word *syllable,* you should recognize that a syllable must contain a vowel sound, diphthong, or syllabic consonant.

It is also difficult to define precisely what is meant by a vowel sound. Various dictionaries agree that the distinguishing feature of a vowel sound is the uninterrupted or nonrestricted outward flow of voiced breath. For vowel sounds, the mouth and throat passages are relatively open, and the vocal folds are vibrating.

The identity of a vowel, as well as its distinctive tone quality, depends on the momentary positioning of the articulators (tongue, lips, jaws, and velum) and on how this positioning modifies the dimensions of the oral cavity and its openings to produce the desired sound. A consonant, on the other hand, is the result of stopping, narrowing, or diverting the breath stream by use of the articulators.

Beginning Drills and Exercises

Before attempting to separate words into their component vowel and consonant sounds, many students find it helpful to engage in vocalized play at combining sounds. The drills and exercises in this chapter are a sample of the type of activity you will be doing for all the phonemes as they are discussed and studied in the chapters to come. The conscientious completion of these drills and exercises should enable you to begin your mastery of phonetics—(1) to sensitize your ears to the individual sounds, or phonemes, which comprise the flow of speech, (2) to free yourself from concentration on the spelling of words, (3) to make the association between sound and phonetic symbol, and (4) to hear your own speech sounds accurately.

---

7. One individual, R. H. Stetson (1951), devoted a great part of his professional life to defining the syllable physiologically. Ladefoged (1958) has also done a lot of work along this line.

8. A discussion of the vocalic *er* sound (appearing in the second syllable of *paternity*) can be found on page 61-62.

Square brackets, which you will notice in the following material, are used to enclose all phonetic transcription,[9] thus separating it from script or printed type. The consonants [p, b, t, d, k, g, f, v, s, z, m, n, h, r, l] appear in phonetic transcription, thereby representing sounds rather than letters. You will note that the phonetic symbols for these consonant sounds are identical to the printed form of the Roman alphabet letters with which these sounds are usually associated. By scanning the table of phonetic symbols on pages 4-5, you will find that other consonant sounds are transcribed with symbols unfamiliar to anyone with no prior knowledge of phonetics. For the time being our transcription will involve only those consonant-sound symbols which are already at our disposal because of their similarity to the printed Roman letters.

The phonemes and those allophonic variations that are considered important are presented in a systematic order in this book. Except in clearly labeled instances, no phoneme will be required in transcription exercises prior to a discussion of how the sound is made. The one major exception to this procedure is the series of sounds just presented. A discussion of how they are formed will be delayed temporarily to enable you to start phonetic transcription immediately.

DRILL

Start with the vowel sound [i] in the word *east*. Say this sound several times, [i i i i i]. Aloud, form syllables by preceding this [i] sound with the sounds usually associated with the consonants *p, b, t, d, k, g, f, v, s, z, l, m, n, r, w,* and *h.* Thus,

[pi]   *pea*

[bi]   *bee*

[ti]   *tea*

[di]   D (the fourth letter of the alphabet)

[ki]   *key*

[gi]   (the word *geese* minus the final *s* sound)

[fi]   *fee*

[vi]   V (the letter preceding *w* in the alphabet)

[si]   *see*

[zi]   Z (the last letter of the alphabet)

9. Various specialists whose work requires a symbolic visual representation of speech sounds make a distinction between phonemes and allophones in their transcription systems. They do this by enclosing phonemic symbols in slant lines within an orthographic text – for example, "the phoneme /i/." Allophones, on the other hand, are enclosed in square brackets []. In this book we will not attempt to distinguish between every phonemic and allophonic illustration, but will use square brackets for both, except where it becomes necessary to show a definite distinction.

[li]	*lee*
[mi]	*me*
[ni]	*knee*
[ri]	(the word *read* minus the final *d* sound)
[wi]	*we*
[hi]	*he*

Now, form syllables beginning with the sound [i] and terminating with the same series of consonants—[ip ib it id ik ig] etc. Reread this list aloud. Did you have any trouble with the last three consonants, [r], [w], and [h]? Can you tell why? The reasons will probably be clearer when you reach the discussions of the formation of [h], [w], and [r] on pages 34 and 35.

Now place the same consonants before and after the vowel sound—[pip bib tit did] etc. Read the list aloud a second time.

You are now ready to try different consonants in a single syllable—[pib bip tid dit pit tip pid dip] etc. In the space provided, write and *simultaneously sound aloud* a long list of such syllables using the vowel [i] and these consonant sounds: [p, b, t, d, k, g, f, v, s, z, l, m, n, r, h].

_____

_____

_____

_____

_____

DRILL ANALYSIS

By this time, the sound [i] should evoke an almost unconscious arm movement producing the dotted symbol which we use to represent this sound phonetically. When you say or hear the sound [i], do you immediately visualize this dotted symbol? If not, you need to repeat the preceding drills and fill several sheets of paper with syllables. However, such paper and pencil work is of little use unless you say the sound as you write it. This technique helps establish the symbol kinesthetically (see G.I.). By this we mean your muscles become accustomed to reacting with a set series of movements when you say or hear a given sound. When you succeed in building a sound into your *kinesthesia*, or muscle sense, writing the correct symbol in response to a particular sound will be about as automatic as saying the word *up* when you're asked to respond immediately with the opposite of *down*.

DRILL

Try this same procedure with the sound [ɪ] as in *hit*. Say the following aloud:

[ɪ   ɪ   ɪ   ɪ   ɪ   ɪ

pɪ bɪ tɪ dɪ kɪ gɪ fɪ vɪ sɪ zɪ mɪ nɪ hɪ rɪ lɪ

ɪp ɪb ɪt ɪd ɪk ɪg ɪf ɪv ɪs ɪz ɪm ɪn ɪr ɪl

pɪp bɪb tɪt dɪd kɪk gɪg fɪf vɪv sɪs zɪz mɪm nɪn

pɪb bɪp tɪd dɪt pɪt tɪp kɪp pɪk bɪk kɪb kɪt], etc.

Now write two lines of syllables using the sound [ɪ] and these same consonant sounds:

_____

_____

DRILL ANALYSIS

Have these drills helped establish firmly the second vowel sound, the [ɪ]? When you hear this sound, do you automatically visualize a straight line with two crossbars? If not, did you visualize the symbol *every* time you said and wrote it? If you slip into the practice of writing these symbols automatically while letting your mind wander, you are wasting your time. This type of drill is effective only as long as you think, say, hear, and write as one operation. The minute your attention wanders, stop! Force your attention back or do something else until you are really ready to concentrate again.

DRILL

You are now ready to contrast the [i] and [ɪ] sounds. Read aloud the following, listening carefully to the contrast between these two vowel sounds:

[i   ɪ   i   ɪ   ɪ   ɪ   i   ɪ   i   ɪ

bi   pɪ   tɪ   ti   pi   pɪ

it   ɪt   ɪb   ib   in   ɪn

bib bɪb pɪp pip dɪd did kik kɪk gig gɪg]

EXERCISE 1

Now you can test yourself to see how well you have learned the first two vowel sounds. Read aloud each of the following sound combinations. If the syllable constitutes a legitimate word, write that word in the blanks provided. Indicate all nonsense syllables by writing X after the phonetics:

Syllable   **Word**

1. [pip] _peap_

2. [bib] _beep_

3. [bit] _beat_

4. [bɪt] _bit_

5. [pɪp] _pip_

6. [bip] _beap_

7. [bɪb] _bib_

8. [bid] _bead_

9. [bɪp] _pid_

10. [pɪb] _____

11. [pit] _____

12. [pɪt] _____

13. [tip] _____

14. [tɪp] _____

15. [dit] _____

16. [tid] _____

17. [drɪp] _____

18. [dip] _____

19. [pɪd] _pid_

20. [pid] _pead_

21. [kit] _____

22. [kɪt] _____

23. [kɪb] _____

24. [gib] _____

25. [gɪt] _____

26. [kɪd] _____

27. [pɪg] _____

28. [frɪb] _____

29. [frɪt] _____

30. [tif] _____

31. [trf] _____

32. [vɪm] _____

33. [mid] _____

34. [mim] _meer_

35. [mit] _meet_

36. [mɪn] _men_

37. [mɪf] _____

38. [min] _____

39. [mɪt] _____

40. [mil] _____

41. [vil] _____

42. [vɪm] _____

43. [sɪn] _____

44. [sin] _____

45. [sid] _____

46. [sɪd] _____   55. [nɪt] _____   64. [lɪp] _____

47. [sɪb] _____   56. [nit] _____   65. [lip] _____

48. [sɪp] _____   57. [tin] _____   66. [lid] _____

49. [sip] _____   58. [tim] _____   67. [lin] _____

50. [pis] _____   59. [tɪm] _____   68. [lɪn] _____

51. [piz] _____   60. [tɪn] _____   69. [lɪm] _____

52. [biz] _____   61. [sit] _____   70. [lim] _____

53. [zɪp] _____   62. [tiz] _____   71. [lɪl] _____

54. [zip] _____   63. [tis] _____   72. [lɪd] _____

EXERCISE 1: DISCUSSION

After you have completed the above exercise, check your work against
the following key:

1. peep	23. X	45. seed, cede
2. X	24. X	46. Sid
3. beet, beat	25. X	47. sib
4. bit	26. kid	48. sip
5. pip	27. pig	49. seep
6. beep	28. fib	50. piece, peace
7. bib	29. fit	51. peas
8. bead	30. X	52. bees
9. X	31. tiff	53. zip
10. X	32. vim	54. X
11. peat, Pete	33. mead	55. knit, nit
12. pit	34. X	56. neat
13. X	35. meet, meat, mete	57. teen
14. tip	36. Min	58. team, teem
15. X	37. miff	59. Tim
16. teed	38. mean	60. tin
17. dip	39. mitt	61. seat
18. deep	40. meal	62. tease, teas, tees
19. X	41. veal	63. X
20. X	42. vim	64. lip
21. X	43. sin	65. leap
22. kit	44. seen, scene	66. lead (verb)

67. lean, lien	69. limb, limn	71. Lil
68. Lynn	70. X	72. lid

You may have noticed that the phonetic transcriptions of *Pete, Min, Sid, Tim, Lynn,* and *Lil* in Exercise 1 did not begin with oversize symbols to indicate capitalization. A sound cannot be capitalized. The asterisk [*] has been used by phoneticians as a prefix to show that the following word is a proper name. Such use of this symbol in the preceding exercise might have helped you recognize the names (or nicknames) [pit], [mɪn], [sɪd], [tɪm], [lɪn], and [lɪl]. However, since proper names can usually be identified easily when words are transcribed in context, this symbol is unnecessary and will not be used in this text to designate proper names.[10]

If some of your errors in Exercise 1 were due to vocabulary difficulties, this may be a good time to add a few words to your vocabulary. However, other errors may appear stupid to you as soon as you consult the answers. In that case, perhaps your study technique included some mental woolgathering. Since undivided attention is necessary, you should divide your study time into many periods of short duration. Few of us are able to maintain the degree of concentration required for rapid gains if we work for long, uninterrupted periods of thirty minutes or more.

EXERCISE 2

Write the following words in phonetics:

1. bill ⌐bɪl⌐	8. feel ⌐fil⌐	15. spill _____
2. pill ⌐pɪl⌐	9. fill ⌐fɪl⌐	16. speak _____
3. peal ⌐pil⌐	10. veal _____	17. creep _____
4. leap ⌐lip⌐	11. nil _____	18. creek _____
5. leak ⌐lik⌐	12. Neal _____	19. lease _____
6. leave ⌐liv⌐	13. treat _____	20. league _____
7. leaf ⌐lif⌐	14. trill _____	21. lid _____

---

10. Furthermore, it is customary in historical linguistics to use the asterisk to indicate that a transcribed form has not been directly observed but represents a theoretically reconstructed, or indirectly inferred, phonemic diagram of an ancient word form (see Hockett, 1958, page 491).

22. print _____   26. flees _____   30. meal _____

23. preened _____   27. fees _____   31. mill _____

24. please _____   28. fizz _____   32. lean _____

25. fleece _____   29. zeal _____

EXERCISE 2: DISCUSSION

If you have diligently sounded out all of the preceding drills and written the appropriate symbols where required, you are beginning to acquire a feeling of how several sounds are combined to form words. Let us now approach the problem in another manner.

EXERCISE 3

Say the following words aloud, listening carefully to how you sound out the words. Do not permit yourself to picture the spelling of the word. Determine the *number of sounds* in each word, and record the number in the blanks provided:

1. cap _____   5. prune _____   8. hat _____

2. shoe _____   6. socks _____   9. tie _____

3. coat _____   7. skirt _____   10. tax _____

4. glove _____

EXERCISE 3: DISCUSSION

Now, let us analyze your answers. You undoubtedly have indicated three sounds for the word *cap*, since a consonant sound precedes and another follows the vowel sound.

If you have more than two sounds for *shoe*, you need to stop and analyze your mistake. Did the spelling confuse you, or cause you to list an extra vowel sound? There is only one vowel *sound*. Did you recognize that only one sound precedes the vowel sound? If the *sh* caused you to react with two consonant sounds, you are probably being influenced by the spelling rather than the sound. Say this word again, and hang on to the first sound. You will see that only one sound follows the first and that is the vowel sound *oo* or [u].

Now check *coat*. The correct answer is three sounds. Just like *cap*, it consists of one vowel sound preceded and followed by a consonant sound. If your answer was *four*, you are being deceived by the spelling which uses two vowels. Actually there is only one vowel *sound*.

Glove is made up of four sounds. The first sound is a voiced pressure build-up and sudden release in the back of the mouth; the second is made with the tongue tip touching the inside surface of the upper gum ridge. The vowel sound [ʌ] follows. The word ends with a consonant sound [v] forced out between the lower lip and upper teeth.

Prune also has only four sounds; the final letter does not represent a sound.

Socks has four sounds.

Skirt has four sounds also. You may have had trouble with the vowel sound in this one. Because of our spelling training, we are apt to be confused by this word. The vowel sound is *er*, or [ɝ], like the sound following the *h* in *her*. Following this sound is a [t]. A [s] and [k] precede the vowel sound.

Hat should offer no problem. It has three sounds—two consonant sounds surrounding a vowel sound.

Tie may have troubled you. We consider this word to contain only two phonemes. The [t] is followed by the diphthong [aɪ]. A *diphthong* is "a speech sound changing continuously from one vowel to another in the same syllable" (Webster, 1959, p. 234). In phonetics a diphthong is considered as one sound unit, or phoneme. Despite the blended dual-vowel aspect of diphthongs, this book will refer to a diphthong as one sound in order to simplify discussions and exercise instructions. (For a full discussion of diphthongs, see Chapter 7.)

You have probably recorded three sounds for the word *tax*, thinking it ended in a [x] sound. This answer is incorrect. The symbol [x] in the phonetic alphabet does not refer to any sound normally used in American English. Try sounding the word again, and hold on to the final sound. You now are holding on to a [s]. Immediately before this sound you make a [k]. Hence, the word *tax* has four sounds and is transcribed [tæks].

You have now had the opportunity to study some errors frequently made by beginners. You are probably becoming aware that one of the first steps in mastering phonetics is freeing yourself from visual symbols. The more you concentrate on spelling, the more you are apt to become confused about the sounds involved.

EXERCISE 4

Record the number of sounds you make in saying the following words aloud:

1. tree _____   9. man _____   17. screw _____

2. grass _____   10. girl _____   18. saw _____

3. street _____   11. boy _____   19. drill _____

4. sky _____   12. hedge _____   20. male _____

5. house _____   13. tacks _____   21. tax _____

6. car _____   14. plane _____   22. river _____

7. bike _____   15. wrench _____ 23. mail _____

8. store _____   16. hammer _____ 24. plain _____

EXERCISE 4: DISCUSSION

In Exercise 4, did you remember that each diphthong is to be treated as only one sound unit? In addition to the previously mentioned [aɪ] – in *sky* and *bike* – the diphthong [aʊ] appears in the word *house*, and the diphthong [ɔɪ] appears in the word *boy*. What did you do with *hedge*? This word ends with the phoneme [dʒ]. While this appears to be two symbols, it actually is similar to the diphthongs in that it functions distinctively as a two-sound combined form. In this case, two consonant sounds merge to form a single phoneme. Like the diphthongs, this phoneme, as well as [tʃ] and [hw], will be considered, for convenience, as one sound. The only words in the left-hand column which do not contain three sounds are *grass* and *store* (four sounds each), and *street* (five sounds). The words in the middle and right-hand columns which do not contain *four* sounds are *boy* and *saw* (two sounds each), and *man, girl, hedge, male,* and *mail* (three sounds each). In checking your work, be sure that you hear the same number of sounds in *male* and *mail*, in *plane* and *plain*, and in *tacks* and *tax*. If your answers differed on the number of sounds within each of these pairs, go back and sound out each word. You will note that each pair of words is sounded identically.

EXERCISE 5

Sound out the following words. Then reverse the order of the sounds, saying them backward. Do not try to spell the word backward; the *sounds* are to be reversed. If sounding backward creates another legitimate word, list the new word: for example, meat *team*, ape *pay*, etc.

1. moot _____	6. cadge _____	11. dates _____
2. wreck _____	7. crop _____	12. file _____
3. tick _____	8. stun _____	13. stone _____
4. note _____	9. talk _____	14. rip _____
5. car _____	10. prune _____	15. crick _____

EXERCISE 5: DISCUSSION

Do you have more than two blanks in this exercise? If so, you need to restudy the remaining blanks. No legitimate words are created by reversing the sounds in numbers 10 and 15, unless you accept a Scottish pronunciation for number 15. Be sure that in reversing the sounds of *crop* you do not end with "a type of meat." If you do, you are having *visual-vowel* trouble. What did you do with *wreck*?

EXERCISE 6

Which of the following words contain other than four sounds? Mark the number of sounds contained in the exceptions:

1. canoe _____	10. hawk _____	19. trout _____
2. crawl _____	11. deep _____	20. dusk _____
3. after _____	12. fox _____	21. bones _____
4. hammock _____	13. birds _____	22. killer _____
5. tired _____	14. water _____	23. flapper _____
6. phlegm _____	15. woods _____	24. hammer _____
7. cruise _____	16. rifle _____	25. occur _____
8. lynx _____	17. stove _____	26. flaccid _____
9. badger _____	18. tent _____	27. million _____

28. essay _____   30. apple _____   32. buzzing _____

29. assert _____   31. rudder _____   33. stutter _____

EXERCISE 6: DISCUSSION

If you have more or less than four exceptions in the first twenty-two words, you need to continue sounding out these words. The exceptions include numbers 10 and 11 (three phonemes each), and numbers 4 and 8 (five phonemes each). In numerical order, the number of sounds for words 23 through 33 is as follows: five, four, three, seven, six, three, four, three, four, five, five.

EXERCISE 7

Circle the words which do *not* contain the [i] sound:

conceit   aggrieve   phoebe   queen   cede

succeed   people   each   key   quest

EXERCISE 7: DISCUSSION

Only the last word should be circled. Notice that Exercise 7 gives eight different spellings for the sound [i]. Phonetics, however, is not subject to such vagaries of spelling. The symbol [i] is used to designate the vowel sound in such words as *feet* and *key* and will never be used to refer to any other sound.

Study Suggestions

You have begun to develop a new skill. You are learning to recognize the individual sounds identifiable in a flow of speech and to transcribe them immediately into visual symbols—the phonetic alphabet. You should have little difficulty in acquiring this new system of notation if you conscientiously complete the drills and exercises in this book. Here are some hints for establishing sound and symbol associations:

1. As each new sound is presented in this book, listen carefully to your instructor's pronunciation of the sound. Imitate him by immediately saying the sound aloud. Look at the symbol which represents this sound. Make the sound again while writing the symbol. Do this several times.

2. Immediately after your phonetics class, repeat this process several times. Visualize the symbol; then say the sound while writing the symbol. Get the feel of the movement necessary to write the symbol. For example, with the sound [i] get the muscular sense or the kinesthetic awareness of making a short downward line with a short curved tail and putting a dot above it. Always say the sound as you write it. Do this while walking to and from classes. Concentrate on the arm and hand movement even though you are not recording the symbol with pencil or pen. Visualize the symbol; feel your arm and hand describing the symbol; simultaneously listen to yourself saying the sound aloud while getting the feel of it on your lips and tongue. In other words, concentrate on the *feedback* (see G. I.) of sensations both from your vocal apparatus and your writing apparatus. At the same time, reinforce these different feedback mechanisms by listening to yourself. In essence, you should attempt to become highly conscious of all the messages sent back to you as you say, write, and hear a sound, just as a baby is presumed to listen to and evaluate his attempts to master our spoken language.

3. Put a card on which you have written the symbol in a prominent place on your study desk. If you remind yourself daily with one symbol in such a fashion, and say the sound it represents each time you see the reminder, the repetition can hardly help but fix the sound (and symbol) in your memory. The next day switch to a new sound and symbol.

4. Follow the above suggestion and plant contrasting symbols, such as [i] and [ɪ] on successive days. Whenever your eye catches the symbols, say the sounds aloud.

5. Be sure, of course, that you attach the correct sound to a given symbol from the very beginning. This is the function of the key words suggested on pages 6-7. (First you need to have your instructor sound them all for you.) It is important to stop using the key words as soon as possible. The techniques listed above should help establish an instantaneous relationship between the sound heard and the phonetic symbol. The faster you stop all references to key words, the quicker you will master phonetics.

6. Another useful technique is that which you used at the beginning of this chapter—the practice of nonsense syllables. Take the symbols [p, b, t, d, k, g, s, z, f, v, l, m, n, r, w, h], which are already familiar to you, and combine them with the vowel sound you are learning. For example, say aloud while writing [ki gi si zi fi vi li mi], etc., then [ip ib it id ik ig], etc., then [pip pib pit pik bip bib bit tik tiz], etc. When you learn another vowel, use this same technique in contrasting the sounds: [pi pɪ pip pɪp bɪp bip bit bɪt], etc. Always listen to yourself as you say the sounds; transcribe them simultaneously, and become aware of the motion required both to say and to write them. This type of concentrated effort at the beginning of your study of phonetics should greatly simplify your study later. It will help you discover the fascination and fun of detecting and identifying sounds we make while talking. Such pleasure in learning can lead to great dividends for you, especially in the improvement of your own articulation and pronunciation.

Before your transcription habits become too thoroughly ingrained and change-resistant, you should be cautioned about the matter of precision in the formation of your phonetic symbols. Carelessly formed symbols can sometimes result in one sound being mistaken for another. Observe carefully the matter of size and space relationships of the symbols to the line of writing.

Many students have found it helpful to visualize an imaginary vowel-line about half as high as the highest symbols—[d], [f], and [l], for example. The tops of vowel symbols extend about half as high above the line of writing as do the tops of the consonant symbols just mentioned. Similarly, the tails of consonants extend about the same distance below the line of writing as the vowels extend above. This imaginary vowel-line is shown below as a dotted line. Illustrated with the [i] symbol are the various consonants discussed thus far:

i p b t d k g s z f v l m n r w h

You will note that the tail-less consonants, such as [s], [z], [v], etc., extend the same distance above the line as do the vowels. About the only symbol that deviates from these relative heights is the [k] which usually is transcribed about three quarters as high as the [d], [f], and [l]. While such precision of measurement is not mandatory, keeping these rules of thumb in mind while transcribing will help minimize the problems of symbol identity.

Short crooks on the bottoms of [i], [t], and [g] are recommended to minimize confusion in rapid transcription. Further guides to symbol formation will be presented when the sounds for which they stand are discussed.

You are now armed with a variety of study techniques. Use them to augment the exercises and drills in this book.

Chapter Summary

[ɪf] you [hæv] studied this chapter carefully, [ju] should be [ebḷ] to define [ðiz] terms—[fənɛtɪks], experimental phonetics, applied phonetics, [fonim], allophone, the IPA, articulation, diacritical [mɑrks], syllable, vowel, [kɑnsənənt], kinesthetic awareness, [fidbæk], and initiating and terminating consonants. You [ʃud] be able to explain [hwʌt wi min] by distinctively different, formal and informal [spitʃ], and dialect areas (or speech regions). [ɪn] addition to this [besɪk] knowledge, you should have begun acquiring (or improving) [ðə faləwɪŋ skɪlz]—recognizing individual [spitʃ saʊndz] or phonemes, dividing [wɝdz] into their respective phonemes, associating speech sounds with their appropriate [fənɛtɪk sɪmbḷz], and transcribing [spitʃ ɪn fənɛtɪk sɪmbḷz].

chapter **2**

SOME CONSONANT SOUNDS

Articulation and its mechanism
The formation of
[p, b, t, d, k, g, m, n, f, v, s, z, l, h, w, r]
Classification of these sounds
according to place and manner of articulation
Aspiration
Dentalization
Voicing and unvoicing
Velopharyngeal closure
Exploded stops (plosives) and unreleased stops
Allophonic versus phonemic transcription
Homorganic sounds
The glottal stop

Articulation and Its Mechanism

In the study of phonetics we need to understand the process of sound articulation. The organs of articulation, or *articulators*, include the tongue, lips, jaws, and velum. In the process of articulation these organs move together to interrupt or constrict the breath stream. In this context Miller (1951, p. 16) has explained articulation as the process of adjusting the shape of the path of the breath stream from the larynx out through the mouth and nose. Let us take a look at the gross anatomy involved in this process.[1]

In Figure 2 we can trace the flow of air upward through the *trachea* (or windpipe), through the vocal folds of the *larynx* (the organ of voice), and through the *pharynx* (throat). The raising and lowering actions of the soft palate (*velum*), along with the contractions of the muscular walls of the pharynx, determine whether the air stream can proceed into the oral cavity (and out past the

---

1. Appendix A presents a greatly simplified discussion of respiration, phonation, and resonation as processes of the speech mechanism.

teeth and lips), or into the nasal cavity (and out through the nostrils), or into both simultaneously.

An aspect of oral anatomy important to the phonetician, but difficult to represent visually, is the relationship of the upper muscles of the pharynx to the velum. The back and side walls of the pharynx are muscular. These muscles contract in a sphincterlike movement which assists the raised velum in closing off the nasal cavity from the oral cavity. This action is called *velopharyngeal closure*.

You will note in Figures 2 and 3 that the roof of the mouth consists of both a *hard* and *soft palate*. If you will run your finger back along the roof of your mouth, you will feel a bony substructure under the mucous membrane. After your finger has passed roughly two thirds of the way back, you will note that the bony substructure ends, and only the soft membranous roof remains. This back

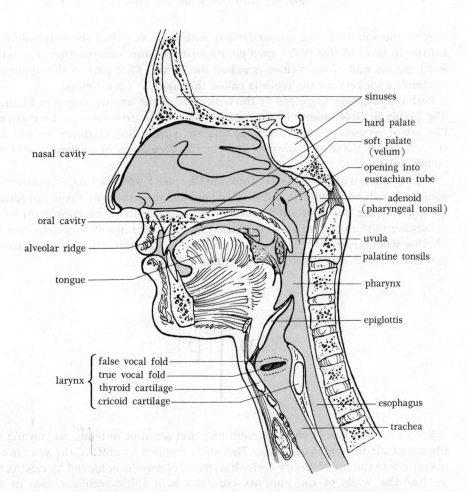

Fig. 2. Median sagittal section showing the nose, mouth, pharynx, larynx, and trachea.

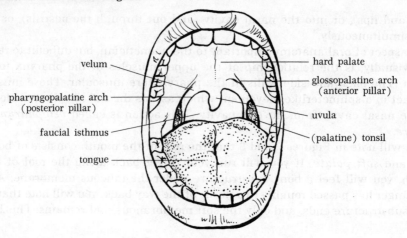

velum

hard palate

glossopalatine arch
(anterior pillar)

pharyngopalatine arch
(posterior pillar)

uvula

faucial isthmus

(palatine) tonsil

tongue

Fig. 3.   Front view of the oral cavity.

part of the mouth's roof not underlaid with bone is called the soft palate, or
velum. In front of this is the *hard palate* with the bony substructure. The hang-
ing terminal end of the velum is called the *uvula*. That part of the upper jaw
containing sockets for the teeth is called the *alveolar* (gum) *ridge*.

Perhaps you were surprised by the bulky size of the tongue shown in Figure 2.
The highly flexible tongue is of prime importance in articulation; the teeth and
lips are of secondary importance. In this and succeeding chapters we will note
the vital part these articulators play in the formation of various vowel and
consonant sounds.

In practicing with nonsense syllables in Chapter 1, you used sixteen consonant
sounds. It will be helpful to familiarize yourself with the way these are formed
before studying any additional sounds. We shall classify each consonant sound
according to the place of its articulation and the manner of its production, including whether or not it is voiced. By following the instructions in this chapter
you should be able to master these sounds quickly.

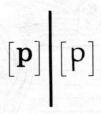

Keep your lips firmly shut momentarily and attempt to blow, preventing the
escape of air through your nose. The air is trapped by closing the pharyngeal
opening into the nasal cavity. Velopharyngeal closure is achieved by raising the
velum. The walls of the pharynx constrict in a sphincterlike action as the
velum is raised, bringing the back wall of the throat slightly forward and moving

the side walls of the throat inward. The meeting of velum and pharyngeal walls closes the velopharyngeal port (see G. I.). These combined actions trap the breath and increase the pressure within the oral cavity. Now quickly open your lips. The resulting outward burst of previously trapped air makes a little explosive sound which we signify by the symbol [p], as in the word *pay*.

Because of the explosive manner in which this sound is produced, it is classified as a *plosive*. Sometimes, however, the explosion phase of such a sound is omitted. In words such as *rib, rude,* and *back*, it is possible to transmit your meaning without exploding the final sound. Such a sound is called an *unreleased stop*. It might be said that no consonant sound is made, but we *infer* the sound from hearing the on-glide (see G.I.), or the way in which the preceding vowel sound was terminated. The place of stoppage influences the preceding vowel quality in such a way that the intended consonant sound is perceived. The more inclusive term *stop* is given to these two types of consonant sounds – exploded and unreleased. The production of a stop depends upon a momentary complete closure of the vocal tract. Since the matter of release (explosion) or nonrelease does not involve a meaning change, we view the unreleased stop as an allophonic variation which need not be differentiated in transcription.

In addition to the manner of formation, or *how* consonants are produced, we also classify them in terms of the place of articulation, or *where* the sound acquires its identifying characteristics (the point of narrowing or contact between articulators). Since [p] is stopped by the two lips, we classify it as a *bilabial* (two-lip) sound.

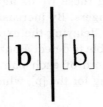

Again, follow the instructions for forming [p], simultaneously vibrating your vocal folds. The resultant sound is no longer [p], but [b], as in *bay*. The only difference in the production of these sounds is the matter of *voicing*, or vocal fold vibration. Hence [p] is a voiceless, bilabial stop, while [b] is a voiced, bilabial stop. We call these two sounds *cognates* because their manner of production is similar. They differ in terms of *voicing* (which yields another means of classification) and sometimes in terms of *aspiration*.

When a strong puff of air accompanies the explosion, the voiceless plosives are called *aspirates* to indicate the breathiness of production. Aspiration occurs when the voiceless plosive begins a stressed syllable, as in *pill* and *appeal*. It does not occur in *spill* or *apple*, since in both cases the sound does not initiate the stressed syllable. The cognate [b] is always unaspirated.

Aspiration is designated in allophonic transcription by a small h [ʰ] written above the line of writing and after the aspirated sound. For example, [pʰɪl] or [tʰɪl]. The word *allophonic* is used here in contrast to *phonemic* and indicates a transcription reflecting specific nondistinctive variants (allophones) of a phoneme. In this book we will use the terms *allophonic* and *phonemic* instead of the more widely used terms *close* (or *narrow*) and *broad* transcription.

DRILL

Perhaps the matter of voicing will become clearer to you if you repeat aloud the following pairs of words, concentrating on the first sound in each pair:

pill, bill	palm, balm	post, boast
peek, beak	putt, but	Paul, ball
paste, based	perch, birch	pie, buy
pen, Ben	poodle, boodle	pout, bout
pack, back	pull, bull	poi, boy

DRILL ANALYSIS

Did you hear the differences in the initial sounds of the above word pairs? If not, try saying these words again. This time, however, close your ears with your fingers. By increasing the length of the pressure build-up stage (thereby delaying the explosion of the initial consonant sound), you should be able to detect a buzzing in your ears for the initial sound in the second word of each pair. This is the voiced [b] sound. You will hear no buzzing for the [p], which is unvoiced.

If you are still not sure that you *hear* the voiced-voiceless difference, perhaps the *f* and *v* word pairs on page 31 will help make this distinction clear to you. Unlike the [p] and [b], the [f] and [v] sounds are not stops and therefore can be prolonged or sustained without changing their essential nature.

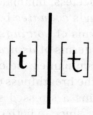

Repeat the procedure for forming [p], but instead of momentarily trapping the air by holding the lips together, trap the air by placing the tongue on the surface of the alveolar (gum) ridge just behind the upper teeth. What sound do you hear as a result of the explosion from this position of your articulators? If you follow the instructions closely, you should hear [t], as in the word *tip*.

Note the puff of air accompanying the explosion. Like the [p], the [t] is aspirated when it initiates a stressed syllable. In most languages, [t] is *dentalized* — that is, it is made by placing the tongue on the teeth rather than on the alveolar ridge. Hence most foreigners need to be taught to raise the level of tongue contact for this sound (as well as for [d], [n], and [l]). In English, [t] and [d] are dentalized only when they are part of a consonant cluster (see G.I.) followed by *th*, as in *eighth* and *width*. We designate dentalization by placing [̪] below the symbol, thus [t̪].

Like the voiceless [p] described above, the [t] also has a voiced cognate. What is it? If in doubt, follow the same instructions which resulted in [t], but vibrate your vocal folds at the same time. The result should be a [d] sound, as in *dip*. It is unaspirated. Thus, in terms of place and manner of production, the voiced [d] and voiceless [t] are both alveolar stops.

A *voiced* [t] is becoming more and more common in the daily speech of educated people in various sections of the United States. It is probably most familiar in words such as *butter* and *bitter*, which frequently are pronounced almost the same as *budder* and *bidder*. Similarly, we find it increasingly difficult to differentiate between the pronunciations of *atom* and *Adam*. A small *v* [t̬] can be used in transcription to designate voicing of a normally voiceless sound.

It is possible that the pronunciations above could be explained on the basis of aspiration, rather than substitution of a voiced sound for its unvoiced cognate. Hence, we might simply be interpreting an unaspirated [t] as a voiced [d].

DRILL

The following list of word pairs is presented for oral and aural practice, although the plosive nature of [t] and [d] like the [p] and [b], makes it difficult to hear the contrast in voicing. Say these words aloud, listening to the difference between the initial sounds of each pair:

team, deem	tab, dab	tuck, duck
tint, dint	tot, dot	Turk, dirk
tail, dale	time, dime	tune, dune
tent, dent	tout, doubt	toes, doze

Two more consonant sounds in our language result from complete stoppage of the breath stream. Do you know which sounds they are? Try the pressure build-up again, this time creating the temporary barrier by bringing the back of the tongue up to the velum while keeping the velopharyngeal port closed. Now quickly release the pressurized air through your mouth. The aspirated explosion from this position far back in your mouth is perceived as the sound [k], as in *coat*.

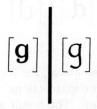

What is the voiced cognate of [k]? Again, you have only to add voicing to (and refrain from aspirating) the [k] sound. The result should be [g], as in *goat*. Hence in terms of our classification system, we say that [k] is a voiceless, velar (see G. I.) stop (which is sometimes aspirated), while its cognate [g] is a voiced, unaspirated, velar stop.

DRILL

The following word list contrasts the [k] and [g] sounds. Remember, the only difference between the initial sounds in each word pair is that of voicing. Say aloud the following pairs:

kill, gill	cuff, guff	curd, gird
kale, gale	cause, gauze	cool, ghoul
cap, gap	came, game	could, good
cot, got	call, gall	coal, goal

Like [p] and [t], [k] is not aspirated in all phonetic contexts. When the sound immediately following any of these phonemes is *homorganic*, they lose their plosive character. Homorganic sounds are those which are made at the same place of articulation but differ in one or more other features of production.

Thus, in the phrases *big car, hip bone,* and *sit down,* the stop sounds at the end of the first word in each pair are not released with aspiration. (The difference between each pair of adjacent homorganic sounds just cited is one of voicing.)

Similarly, [p], [t], and [k] are not aspirated when followed by [m], [n], and [l]. When followed by [m] and [n], the stop sounds are released through the nasal passages, as in *upmost, eaten,* and *lightning.* In the case of an [l] following one of the three voiceless stops, an unaspirated (or weakly aspirated) release of air is made laterally over the sides of the tongue, as in *witless, rippling,* and *sparkler.* Generally speaking, the voiceless stops are strongly aspirated when preceding stressed vowels and weakly aspirated or unaspirated when terminating a syllable or when initiating an unstressed syllable.

The voiced consonant stops [b], [d], and [g] also are altered in certain phonetic contexts. They tend to be unvoiced when they immediately precede other voiceless consonants and when they begin or end a phrase.

DRILL

Read the following phrases aloud, listening carefully to the sounds corresponding to the underscored letters:

1. Bob was rude.

2. Did you dig?

3. He was absent.

Could you detect the unvoicing in each of these examples? At the ends of phrases, both released (exploded) and unreleased forms of the voiced stops are heard.

One additional stop sound, while it is not a distinctive speech sound in English, is heard in the speech of many Americans. This is the *glottal stop.* In phonetic transcription, this sound is represented by an undotted question mark [ʔ]. The sound results from the sudden release of air pressure built up in the trachea. Stoppage takes place at the glottis (the space between the vocal folds), where the air is momentarily trapped by complete closure of the vocal folds.

An exaggerated form of this sound is heard in the explosive release heard in coughing. The glottal stop is most frequently heard as a prefix to an initial vowel sound which is either emphatically or hesitantly uttered. It is also sometimes heard as a substitute for [t] in such words as *bottle* and *little.* Occasional use of this sound will usually go unnoticed, but frequent use may distract the listener by disturbing the rhythmic flow of the speaker's words.

Kenyon (1950, p, 47) recognizes an unexploded form of the glottal stop. As in the case of unreleased allophones [p], [t], and [k], this stop sound is inferred from the influence the vocal fold cut-off has on the preceding vowel.

$$[\mathbf{m,n}]\ \big|\ [m,n]$$

Our language incorporates other sounds made at the same places of articulation as the six sounds just mentioned, but produced in different ways. Close the lips as you do to produce the sound [b]. Instead of exploding the voiced air, lower the velum and send the vocalized air out through the nose in a steady stream. What sound are you making? Your answer should be [m], as in *my*. In terms of manner of production, the voiced bilabial [m] is further classified as a *nasal*, because the air stream escaped through the nasal passages. Thus, [m] is a voiced, bilabial nasal.

In contrast to the stops, [m] is sometimes termed a *continuant*, because it may be prolonged as long as the breath supply lasts. Those who use the word *continuant* generally employ it to refer to all nonstop sounds. This book will not use the term, however, since it does not add any information to that provided by the descriptive words *stop* or *nasal* (already discussed), or by the words *fricative, lateral,* or *glide* (which will be discussed later).

When [m] is preceded by the voiceless consonant [s] in the same syllable, it is sometimes partially unvoiced. Compare, for instance, the [m] in the following word pairs: *mart–smart, mall–small, mere–smear, might–smite.* The [m] in the first word of each pair is more fully voiced than the [m] following the voiceless [s] in the second word. In allophonic transcription this nonvoicing of a normally voiced sound is indicated by placing a small circle under the unvoiced sound—for example, [smɑrt] and [smɪr].

We produce another nasal sound by using the position of closure used for the [d] sound. Send the vocalized air stream through the nose, blocking the oral aperture with the tongue pressed tightly against the alveolar ridge in front and against the inner surfaces of the upper molars. The result, as you should have discovered, is the sound beginning the word *no* and represented by the symbol [n]. Thus [n] is a voiced, alveolar nasal.

Like [t] and [d], [n] is dentalized in most foreign languages. In English, it is dentalized only in combination with *th*, as in *ninth*. Like [m], [n] is sometimes partially unvoiced when following a voiceless consonant in the same syllable. Note the fuller voicing of the [n] in the first word of each of the following word pairs: *knack–snack, near–sneer, knob–snob, no–snow.*

DRILL

Just as the contrasts of [p] and [b], [t] and [d], and [k] and [g] distinguish differences of voicing, the initial nasal sounds in the following word pairs should help you note differences due solely to the place of articulation. Say the following words aloud and feel, as well as hear, the difference in the place of articulation:

meet, neat	map, nap	mock, knock
mitt, knit	Maude, gnawed	mutt, nut
maze, neighs	mere, near	moose, noose
met, net	might, night	mode, node

$$[\mathbf{f},\mathbf{v}] \;\Big|\; [\mathsf{f},\mathsf{v}]$$

With the velopharyngeal port closed, bring your lower lip into light contact with the edges of your upper front teeth and force unvocalized air between these two structures. The resultant sound [f], as in *fame*, is the audible friction of the narrowly constricted breath stream. This friction in the sound's production results in our classifying the sound as a *fricative*. How will we classify the sound in terms of where it is made? Since this sound's identifying characteristics are based on the contact of lip and teeth, we call the sound a *labiodental* (from *labio*, derived from *labium* meaning "lip," and *dental*, pertaining to teeth).

Follow the instructions for making [f], and simultaneously vibrate your vocal folds. What sound do you hear yourself making? It should be [v], as in *vein*. The [f] and [v] are made identically except for the absence or presence of voicing. Thus, [f] is a voiceless, labiodental fricative and [v] is a voiced, labiodental fricative.

DRILL

Say the following word pairs, concentrating on the first sound of each word. Note the difference in voicing between the initial sounds:

feel, veal	fend, vend	fast, vast
feign, vein	fault, vault	first, versed

Unlike the stop sounds, the fricatives [f] and [v] can be prolonged without destroying or altering their basic characteristics. Apply to these sounds the ear-plugging test for voicing which you applied to the [p] and [b] sounds. In this instance the difference between the sounds should be very noticeable. Another way to detect the difference between cognates is to firmly grasp the larynx near its top and *feel* the difference between [f] and [v]. While sounding a [v], you can feel the vibrations emanating from the vocal folds. No such vibration can be detected while sustaining a [f].

The sound [v] frequently presents problems to the person whose native language is Spanish, since [b] and [v] are not separate phonemes in the Spanish language. Also, [v] is frequently used for the sound [w], as in *we*, by speakers of Germanic languages. In both these cases, spelling should provide the clues for pronunciation, once the formation of these sounds is clarified by the person interchanging them.

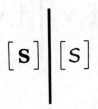

The next sound to be studied is even less easily observed than the ten sounds previously described. The distinguishing characteristics of this sound result from constricting the path of the breath stream within the oral cavity where it is difficult to see and feel the position of the structures during production. The sound is the result of the friction of the unvocalized breath stream traveling down the middle of the top of the tongue through a narrow channel formed by raising the sides of the tongue. It is directed to the alveolar ridge, where it is deflected down and across the cutting edge of the lower front teeth. The velum is raised, closing off the nasal port (see G.I.), and the upper and lower teeth must be in close proximity. The tip of the tongue can be either against the lower gums or behind the upper teeth. (In the latter case, the tip should not touch the teeth or gum ridge.) The resulting voiceless, alveolar fricative is [s], as in *so*.

If the tongue touches the back of the upper teeth while you are making the [s] sound, the acoustic result is called a *dental lisp*. A *protrusion lisp* will occur if the tongue is between the teeth during the production of [s]. Both of these speech defects are sometimes called *frontal lisps*. If, in making [s], the air escapes over the sides of the tongue, the defect is called a *lateral lisp*.

$$[\text{z}]\ [\text{z}]$$

Add voicing to the production of the [s] sound. What do you hear? The cognate produced is [z], as in *zoo*. Hence [z] is a voiced, alveolar fricative.

DRILL

> For practice in differentiating between the cognates [s] and [z], say the
> following word pairs aloud, concentrating on the special characteristics
> of the initial sounds within each pair:

seal, zeal	said, zed	Sue, zoo
sink, zinc	sounds, zounds	sown, zone

> Again, apply both the ear-plugging and larynx-feeling tests to heighten
> your awareness of the voicing differences between [s] and [z].

In addition to the [h] discussed later in this chapter, more fricative consonants will be studied in Chapter 5. Meanwhile, it might be noted that when
voiced fricatives, such as [v] and [z], precede voiceless consonant sounds, or
when they start or end a sentence or phrase, they are partially unvoiced.

DRILL

> You can note this modification by listening carefully to yourselves and
> others saying the following sentences:
>
> 1. Zeros are called ciphers.
> 2. That dive sets my nerves aquiver.
> 3. "Vassar Girl" won the race at twenty-one to five.

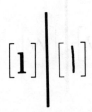

With the velopharyngeal port closed, put the tip of your tongue on the alveolar
ridge. Lower the sides of the tongue, allowing a voiced column of air to pass
through one or both lateral openings. What sound are you making? This is the
voiced, alveolar sound [l], as in *lie*. Some phoneticians refer to [l] as a *glide* —
"a sound produced by an uninterrupted movement of the articulatory mechanism from the position of one sound to that of another" (Kantner and West,
1960, p. 58). This designation applies sometimes to [l] (when it initiates a vowel
sound); however, an [l] which terminates a syllable cannot be considered a glide.
The [l] sound is always correctly termed a *lateral* because, in its production, the
air stream is emitted laterally. In English, [l] is dentalized in combination with

"th," as in *wealth*. Sometimes [l] is partially unvoiced in stressed syllables when it follows voiceless consonant sounds – for example, *plea* and *clip* ([pl̥i] and [kl̥ɪp] in allophonic transcription).

Two [l] allophones are the *light* and the *dark* [l]'s. In general, [l] sounds made with relatively front tongue positions (those followed or accompanied by a high front tongue position) are considered light. The [l] sounds in *leap*, *list*, and *please* are typical light [l]'s. Those [l] sounds made with relatively back tongue positions (those followed by high back tongue positions and those preceding consonant sounds) are dark. Examples of the dark [l] are found in *ball*, *spilled*, and *poll*. Initial [l]'s are usually light; final [l]'s are usually dark.

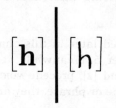

With the velopharyngeal port closed, open your mouth and abruptly exhale a slight puff of unvoiced air. The resulting sound [h], as in *he*, is due to the audible friction of the air stream passing over the edges of the partially closed nonvibrating vocal folds. There is no characteristic mouth position; when producing [h], your mouth assumes the position required by the following vowel sound. The [h] sound is produced in the glottis – the opening between the vocal folds. Thus, the sound is classified as a voiceless, glottal fricative. It is usually heard only at the beginning of stressed syllables.

Pucker your lips to make an *oo* sound, as in *too*. With the articulators in this position, begin vibrating the vocal folds, simultaneously moving the articulators to whatever position is demanded by the following vowel sound. This voiced movement away from the *oo* sound to the position of the following vowel or diphthong sound is designated by the symbol [w], as in *wine*. The [w] is a voiced, bilabial, velar glide. The crucial aspect of this sound's production is its movement, its continual change of position in time.

This sound is partially unvoiced when following a voiceless consonant – particularly a voiceless fricative. The unvoiced [w̥] in the second word of the following word pairs can be contrasted with the fully voiced [w] in the initial word of each pair: *wing – swing*, *wet – sweat*, *wart – thwart*, *wan – swan*.

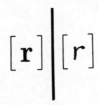

Raise the central portion of the tongue up toward, but not touching, the hard palate, keeping the tongue tip lowered. Begin to vibrate the vocal folds, simultaneously moving from this position into the position required for the following vowel sound. The resulting glide sound is [r], as in *red* or *rabbit*. This [r] is a voiced, palatal (or central) glide. Another [r] allophone can be produced starting from a position in which the tip of the tongue is curled upward, pointing toward the alveolar ridge. In this case, we call the resultant [r] a voiced, alveolar glide, or the *retroflex r*.

Chapter Summary

[ðə tʃif em əv ðis tʃæptɚ] was to help you understand how [sɪkstin kɑnsənənt saʊndz] are formed. [ðis ɪnfɚmeʃən] can perhaps be summarized best [ɪn tʃart fɔrm]. [ɪn ðis tʃart ðə ro hɛdɪŋz] indicate the place of [ɑrtɪkjələʃən], and [ðə kɑləm hɛdɪŋz ɪndəket] the manner of production. Within each pairing of symbols, [ðə fɝst əv ðə pɛr ɪz ʌnvɔɪst], whereas [ðə sɛkənd mɛmbɚ əv ðə pɛr ɪz vɔɪst]. Of those sounds not paired, the [h] is unvoiced, while the lateral, [ðə nezəlz], and [ðə glaɪdz] are voiced. In addition to understanding these consonant sounds, [ju ʃʊd] be able to identify and [ɪksplen] the function of [ðiz pɑrts əv ðə spitʃ] mechanism—vocal [foldz], larynx, pharynx, hard palate, [viləm], alveolar ridge, oral cavity, tongue, [tiθ], lips, and nasal cavity.

Some American English Consonant Sounds

	Stops	Fricatives	Nasals	Laterals	Glides
Bilabial	[p b]		m		w
Labiodental		f v			
(Lingua-)Alveolar[2]	t d	s z	n	l	r
(Lingua)Palatal[2]					r
(Lingua)Velar[2]	k g				
Glottal		h]			

2. The prefix *Lingua-* indicates use of the tongue in the formation of the sound. Although these forms are commonly called alveolar, palatal, and velar for the sake of brevity, the formal designations are lingua-alveolar, linguapalatal, and linguavelar.

chapter 3

THE FRONT VOWELS

Cardinal vowels
Vowel charts
The formation of [i, ɪ, e, ɛ, æ, a]
Tense and lax vowels
Diphthongs [ɪi] and [eɪ]
Troublesome words

In this chapter we will discuss the manner of producing the front vowels [i], [ɪ], [e], [ɛ], [æ] and the front-central [a], plus certain allophonic variations of these phonemes. Front vowels are those formed by raising the front of the tongue toward the front part of the palate.

Except in whispered speech, all vowel sounds are voiced—that is, the vocal folds must be in vibration.[1] The vibrating air stream is resonated in the throat, mouth, and, to a certain degree, in the nose. To produce a non-whispered vowel sound, then, we need (1) a sufficiently strong outward flowing breath stream, (2) a vibrator—the vocal folds which help set the air stream into vibration—and (3) a resonator—the pharynx and the oral cavity, and, to some extent, the nasal cavity.

The tongue is extremely important in determining the vowel sound because of its ability to vary the relationship of the oral and pharyngeal divisions of the oralpharyngeal tract (see G.I.). Moreover, the highly flexible tongue can greatly modify or change the slant and height of the floor of the oral cavity. The jaw also aids in increasing or decreasing the vertical dimensions of the mouth cavity, and the positions of the lips, in conjunction with the movements of the jaw, determine the size and shape of the anterior opening.

Tongue positions for English vowels during prolongation have been portrayed graphically in various schema. In 1949 the International Phonetic Association

---

1. The vocal folds do not vibrate during the whispering of vowel sounds. Such sounds are audible because of the friction resulting from forcing the air stream through a narrow laryngeal opening.

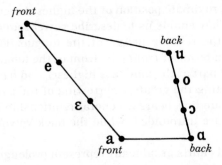

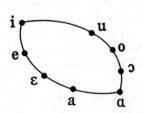

Fig. 4. Diagram illustrating the tongue positions of the eight primary cardinal vowels. The relative positions of the highest points of the tongue are shown by dots.[2]

Fig. 5 A more accurate form of the vowel diagram (Fig. 4).[3]

adopted English phonetician Daniel Jones' conventionalized schema to represent the eight *cardinal vowels*. This figure and its curvilinear counterpart, which Jones says is more scientifically accurate, are reproduced here as Figures 4 and 5.

Wise (1957, p. 84) notes that the word *cardinal* was appropriated from the mariner's nomenclature, in which it refers to the principal directions, or points, on the compass. Phoneticians use it to refer to eight basic vowel positions, which are intended to serve as measurement standards. By defining a cardinal vowel as "a theoretic vowel made with a tongue position that is invariable, easily described in writing or printing so as to be communicable at a distance" (p. 85), Wise is forced to restrict the term *cardinal* to the four vowels at the corners of the diagram, since none of the remaining intermediate sounds can be reproduced invariably with the same tongue position.

The original eight cardinal vowels were judged by Jones (1932, p.32) to have approximately equal "degrees of acoustic separation." He described them, however, in terms of *physiological* positions.[4] Other *intermediate* or *noncardinal* vowels sounds, such as [ɪ], [æ], [ʊ], [ə], and [ɜ], are also recognized by the IPA as having phonemic significance in various languages, including English. Kenyon's 1950 vowel chart, presented here as Figure 6, would seem to be more useful than Jones' charts to the student of American pronunciation.

2. From Daniel Jones, *An Outline of English Phonetics*, 8th ed., page 36. New York: E. P. Dutton & Co., Inc., 1956.
3. *Ibid.*
4. In the late spring of 1925, C. K. Thomas attended a three-week "lectureship" on Phonetics given by Jones at Smith College, Northampton, Massachusetts. In discussing this experience with the author, Thomas recalled that Jones played a phonograph recording of the *cardinal vowels*, which was intended to serve as a standard set of acoustic marking-points for reference by students of various languages, Jones (1932, page 37) notes that the relative positions of cardinal [i], [a], [ɑ], and [u] on his schemata were obtained from X-ray photographs. On page iv of the eleventh edition of Jones' *English Pronouncing Dictionary* is a diagram comparing the tongue positions of "average English vowels" with those of the cardinal vowels.

These various charts illustrate the approximate position of the highest tongue humping for the given vowel sounds. They enable us to describe vowel sounds as *high, mid,* and *low,* depending on the relative height of the tongue. The vowel sounds can be further described in terms of *front* (the front of the tongue is the highest part), *central* (the central part of the tongue is highest), and *back* (the back of the tongue is highest, creating the greatest narrowing of the path of the air stream). The matter of lip rounding bears a general relationship to the tongue positions; the front vowels are unrounded, while the back vowels, except for [ɑ], are rounded.[5]

You should remember that these vowel charts graphically represent prolonged vowel sounds. They have not taken into account the dynamics of flowing speech in which the oral relationships are in a continual state of flux. Obviously, speech does not consist of a succession of discrete articulatory positions or individual sounds placed independently one after the other. While it may be argued that these concepts of tongue humping are artificial because they are nondynamically ascertained, there is some evidence that sustained vowels are not unlike dynamically produced vowels with respect to their acoustical characteristics

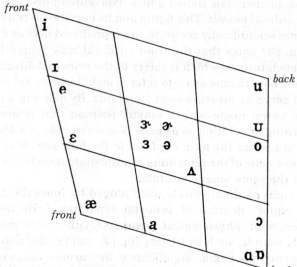

Fig. 6.   Chart of the tongue positions for the vowels.[6]

and their physiological positions. For this reason, and because these concepts seem to be helpful in kinesthetically identifying and orally producing the various vowel sounds, brief descriptions will be given of the static formation of each vowel sound.

It was formerly believed that all sounds other than [m], [n], and [ŋ] – the *ng* sound after the vowel in *sing* – were produced with the velopharyngeal valve

5. This book generally follows Kenyon's categories of front, central, and back. Thomas departs from this classification in that he considers the unround [ʌ] also to be a back, rather than a central, vowel (as does Jones, 1932, page 84).

6. Adapted from John S. Kenyon, *American Pronunciation,* page 61. Ann Arbor, Michigan: George Wahr Publishing Company, 1958.

completely closed. Recent research suggests that the nasal cavity is not completely sealed for most sounds. Instead, it is apparent that some varying but slight amounts of nasal vibration are present in most voiced speech sounds.

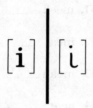

The first vowel sound to be used for extensive transcription practice is the sound [i], as in the words *key, freeze,* and *week.* The [i] is one of the two vowel symbols used for practice in Chapter l.

EXERCISE 8

Transcribe the following words. Do not linger on the visual aspect, or spelling, of the word. Sound it out; then write what you hear:

1. peat _____	14. tease _____	27. seat _____
2. peek _____	15. team _____	28. seed _____
3. piece _____	16. teens _____	29. seek _____
4. peal _____	17. deep _____	30. seize _____
5. peeve _____	18. deed _____	31. cease _____
6. beat _____	19. deal _____	32. seal _____
7. beet _____	20. deem _____	33. seen _____
8. bead _____	21. keep _____	34. zeal _____
9. beak _____	22. keys _____	35. feet _____
10. bees _____	23. keel _____	36. feat _____
11. beef _____	24. keen _____	37. feed _____
12. beam _____	25. geese _____	38. fees _____
13. teak _____	26. seep _____	39. fief _____

40. feel _____	49. meat _____	58. knees _____
41. veal _____	50. mead _____	59. reap _____
42. leap _____	51. meek _____	60. read _____
43. lead _____ (verb)	52. meal _____	61. reek _____
44. leak _____	53. mean _____	62. reef _____
45. lease _____	54. neat _____	63. real _____
46. leaf _____	55. need _____	64. ream _____
47. leave _____	56. knead _____	65. weep _____
48. lean _____	57. niece _____	66. weed _____

EXERCISE 8: DISCUSSION

With the exception of the word *teens* (number 16), all of the above words are made up of three sounds: (1) an initiating consonant, (2) the vowel sound [i], and (3) a terminating consonant.

EXERCISE 9

Circle each of the following words which contains the sound [i]. Do not do this exercise silently; sound aloud each word as you proceed:

1. feed	7. machine	13. deaf	19. Phoenix
2. fed	8. cuisine	14. ideal	20. people
3. feat	9. spring	15. knead	21. indeed
4. feet	10. grievous	16. reason	22. me
5. bleed	11. piece	17. Caesar	23. visa
6. bleat	12. peace	18. creel	24. grief

EXERCISE 9: DISCUSSION

You should not have circled words 2, 9, and 13. Consult your phonetic dictionary if you disagree on number 13.

EXERCISE 10

Circle each of the following words which does *not* contain the sound [i]:

1. steep	7. bleed	12. dill	17. briefs
2. steppes	8. weather	13. yield	18. believe
3. spree	9. deal	14. heat	19. either
4. season	10. dealt	15. heart	20. athlete
5. bleat	11. peal	16. scenes	21. keen
6. bleak			

EXERCISE 10: DISCUSSION

Five or six words should have been circled in this exercise. The word *either* can begin with [i] or with the diphthong [aɪ].

EXERCISE 11

Transcribe the following words:

1. tweed _____	12. dreams _____
2. bleak _____	13. freak _____
3. clique _____	14. green _____
4. flea _____	15. priest _____
5. flee _____	16. scream _____
6. gleam _____	17. streets _____
7. plea _____	18. queen _____
8. sleeps _____	19. tree _____
9. beasts _____	20. skied _____
10. breeds _____	21. sneeze _____
11. creel _____	22. speed _____

23. Steve _____	27. weaves _____
24. Swede _____	28. heaps _____
25. sweep _____	29. greets _____
26. leaves _____	30. squeak _____

EXERCISE 11: DISCUSSION

If you sounded aloud each word before writing it, the above exercise probably caused you no trouble. If you ignored this rule, which is so basic to training yourself in phonetics, you probably had difficulty transcribing *clique, queen,* and *squeak* (numbers 3, 18, and 30). Did you enlarge the [s] symbol to show that *Steve* and *Swede* are capitalized? If so, you should ask yourself how a capital letter changes the *sound* of a word. As you were cautioned earlier, *we do not capitalize in phonetic transcription.* One reason for this rule (aside from that given earlier) is that some of our printed English capital letters, notably G, N, R, and X, are IPA symbols for sounds used in speaking other languages; using these symbols for any other reason might be confusing or misleading. Check your transcription of the endings of *breeds, dreams, leaves,* and *weaves* (numbers 10, 12, 26, and 27). Sound out these words slowly. They all end with [z], not [s].

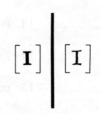

You are now ready to concentrate on another vowel sound—[ɪ] as in *it, pick,* and *Dick.* These key words are given to aid you in your original identification of the sound referred to by the symbol [ɪ]. Have your instructor repeat the sound several times while you listen closely. If you are to acquire any skill in phonetic transcription, you need to go through the various steps suggested in Chapter 1 in order to build an immediate sound-symbol response. Stop using the key words as soon as possible—but be sure that in building your sound-symbol response you are associating the correct symbol with the given sound. Use Exercise 12 to help in this endeavor.

EXERCISE 12

Transcribe the following words:

1. pit _____	22. dim _____	43. sit _____
2. pick _____	23. din _____	44. sick _____
3. pig _____	24. kit _____	45. sieve _____
4. pill _____	25. kid _____	46. sill _____
5. pin _____	26. kick _____	47. sin _____
6. bit _____	27. kiss _____	48. zip _____
7. bid _____	28. kill _____	49. lip _____
8. big _____	29. kin _____	50. lit _____
9. biff _____	30. gig _____	51. lid _____
10. bill _____	31. give _____	52. lick _____
11. bin _____	32. gill _____	53. live _____
12. tip _____	33. fib _____	54. mitt _____
13. tick _____	34. fit _____	55. mid _____
14. tiff _____	35. fig _____	56. miss _____
15. till _____	36. fizz _____	57. mill _____
16. tin _____	37. fill _____	58. nip _____
17. dip _____	38. fin _____	59. knit _____
18. did _____	39. Vic _____	60. nil _____
19. Dick _____	40. vim _____	61. rip _____
20. dig _____	41. sip _____	62. rib _____
21. dill _____	42. sib _____	63. writ _____

64. rid _____	71. his _____	78. win _____
65. rig _____	72. hill _____	79. Lynn _____
66. riff _____	73. him _____	80. Wynn _____
67. rill _____	74. wit _____	81. hymn _____
68. rim _____	75. wick _____	82. built _____
69. hip _____	76. wig _____	83. cyst _____
70. hit _____	77. will _____	84. sylph _____

EXERCISE 12: DISCUSSION

You will note that all but the last three words in the above exercise are made up of only three *sounds* each, even though four or five letters are needed to spell some of them. Note particularly the entirely unnecessary *k* in *knit* and the *w* in *writ*. Silent letters are not indicated in phonetic transcription.

EXERCISE 13

Record in the blank the correct spelling for each of the following phonetically transcribed words:

1. [pɪt] _____	9. [tɪmz] _____
2. [bin] _____	10. [pit] _____
3. [wɪnd] _____	11. [bɪn] _____
4. [wind] _____	12. [fɪst] _____
5. [fist] _____	13. [lip] _____
6. [lɪp] _____	14. [mit] _____
7. [mɪt] _____	15. [rɪl] _____
8. [ril] _____	16. [tɪmz] _____

EXERCISE 13: DISCUSSION

Perhaps you noticed that all of the [i] words in Exercise 13 were paired somewhere in the list with an [ɪ] word transcribed identically except for the vowel sound. Accordingly, any word in your list which is duplicated indicates an error in reading the phonetic transcription.

EXERCISE 14

Transcribe the following:

1. digs _____
2. Dick's _____
3. blitz _____
4. bleats _____
5. bliss _____
6. knead _____
7. sixteen _____
8. scenic _____
9. freeze _____
10. swift _____
11. geese _____

12. peeled _____
13. creek _____
14. creak _____
15. field _____
16. filled _____
17. grist _____
18. greased _____
19. heaved _____
20. wind _____
21. weaned _____
22. brisk _____

Say the sounds [i] and [ɪ] aloud, concentrating on the way in which you produce them. For both sounds, although the tongue tip is normally placed against the back of the lower front teeth, the remaining bulk of the tongue is high in the front of the mouth; this position is higher for [i]. The jaw opening is very narrow for [i] but slightly wider for [ɪ]. The lips are retracted more for [i]; for [ɪ] the lips are more relaxed. For these, as for all vowel sounds, the velum is raised, closing off the nasal cavity.

In addition to describing the English vowels as high—mid—low, and front—central—back, phoneticians designate vowels as *tense* or *lax* on the basis of the degree of muscular tension necessary to produce them. Verification of such a quality as tension, however, is highly subjective. The easiest way to detect this difference in the [i] and [ɪ] sounds is to touch lightly the fleshy portions, or underside, of the tongue muscles (beneath the chin) while alternately saying these two vowel sounds. When saying the tense vowel, you should be able to feel a muscular bulging which is not noticeable when producing the lax vowel.

The first sound in each of the following pairs is generally considered to be tense in contrast to the second: [i]–[ɪ], [e]–[ɛ], [o]–[ɔ], and [u]–[ʊ]. Distinctions in tension are regarded as less certain for the low vowels (made with a lower tongue humping) than for the high vowels (made with the tongue nearer the palate).

Tense vowels tend to be sustained somewhat longer than lax vowels; in addition, they have a diphthongal tendency due to a slight tongue rising. For example, the gliding [ɪi], as in *me*, is an allophone of the phoneme [i]. Since the interchange of [i] and [ɪi] produces no change of meaning in English, the transcriptions in this book will require only the use of the phoneme [i]. The tendency to diphthongize long vowels is more pronounced in the South than elsewhere in the United States.

Few languages other than English use variable muscular tension as a phonemic distinction. Hence concentration on the tension contrasts of such vowels as [i] and [ɪ] is one of the major means by which foreigners learn to produce these vowels in an acceptable fashion.

Attention to the tension contrasts of [i] and [ɪ] might also help resolve some of the transcription problems of words ending with the letter *y*, such as *party*, *daisy*, and *envy*. Many people hear an [i] rather than an [ɪ] allophone at the ends of these words. Kenyon and Knott recognized the occurrence of either [i] or [ɪ] endings but considered it unfeasible to record both for every word ending in *-y*. For convenience, they chose the [ɪ] variant because they thought it was more commonly used in America.

Since the final syllables of words ending in *-y* are invariably unstressed, thereby utilizing lax – rather than tense – vowels, it is possible to stylize phonetic transcription on this basis and to use only the symbol for the lax vowel [ɪ]. However, stylization of this type, while perhaps useful in printing dictionaries, is not necessarily desirable in phonetic (or phonemic) transcription. You should listen intently to these sounds and not stylize what you *think* you *hear* on the basis of what you *believe* you *say*.

You must also recognize that you do not necessarily pronounce a word in context the same as you do when it stands alone. For words ending in *-y* the tongue frequently does not rise all the way forward for the true [i] required for the first sound of the next word. If you begin seriously tuning your ears to continuous connected speech, as contrasted with isolated words, you will begin to hear many more final [ɪ] sounds. Some final *-y* endings, however, never seem to sound like [ɪ]; you will continue to perceive them as the sound [i]. Your instructor might wish to use some type of allophonic (or phonemic) distinction in these cases. To aid you in Chapter 8 and to avoid confusion elsewhere, this text will reflect the Kenyon and Knott transcription, since [i] and [ɪ] can be interchanged without affecting the meaning of words ending in *-y*. Thomas (1958, p. 100) suggests that the final [ɪ] sound in words such as *city* and *easy* is most typical of the pronunciation of older people who have not been affected by the trend toward final [i] sounds which has become evident during the past half century. He also detects a regional regularity in the pronunciation of the final [ɪ] or [i] sounds. The [ɪ] pronunciation, he states, is more common in the South.[7]

To summarize this discussion of the [i] and [ɪ] sounds, we might say that [i] is a high-front, unround (retracted lips) tense sound, while [ɪ] is a high-front, unround, lax sound. All vowels, of course, are voiced.

EXERCISE 15

At a normal rate, read the following sentences aloud, listening carefully to yourself, and transcribe the underscored word as you believe you said it in context:

1. Is it <u>easy</u> or hard? _____

2. He spoke <u>clearly</u> and softly. _____

3. He is a <u>greedy</u> man. _____

4. That's a <u>sneaky</u> thing to do. _____

5. The child was <u>sleepy</u> and cold. _____

6. The <u>treaty</u> was signed. _____

7. She was <u>dreamy</u> eyed. _____

8. The <u>weepy</u> woman cried all night _____

9. What is a <u>Mickey</u> Finn? _____

10. There was a <u>misty</u> expression in her eyes. _____

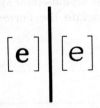

The next vowel sound for us to consider is the sound [e] as in *take, fate,* and *lake.* This is the front vowel just below [ɪ]. The humping of the tongue toward

---

7. Readers wishing to study further analyses of modifications and variations in the use of [i] or [ɪ] are referred to Bronstein (1960, pp. 147-151), to Curtis and Hardy (1959, p. 247), and to Thomas (1958, pp. 61-63).

the front of the mouth is slightly less than that for the sound [ɪ]. The jaw is open wider and the lips are only slightly retracted. Hence we call [e] a mid-front, tense, unround vowel sound.

In our language this sound is usually a *diphthong*. That is to say, it consists of a fusion or blending of two vowel sounds pronounced within a syllable as one vowel unit. This diphthongal characteristic is perhaps best detected in word endings such as *day, play, say,* and *gay.* Although many (perhaps most) [e] sounds are diphthongs, the distinction between the pure (see G. I.) [e] and the diphthong [eɪ] will never distinguish English words otherwise sounded alike. Since the [eɪ] sound is a nonphonemic variant of [e] in our language, it follows that interchanging [e] and [eɪ] will introduce no change of meaning. Accordingly, in this book we will not attempt to distinguish between these sounds, but will use the single symbol [e] to represent all variants of this sound, just as we will use the symbol [i] to represent all the variants of this sound, including the diphthong [ɪi]. However, the person interested in working with dialects—either as an actor, director, or correctionist—needs to be acutely aware of the two sounds [e] and [eɪ]. A rule of thumb for these specialists is that in English the so-called pure vowel [e] is normally found only in unaccented syllables; in accented syllables the [e] sound is usually diphthongized to [eɪ]. (In allophonic or close transcription *vacation* would be transcribed [vekeɪʃən].) An exception to this rule is the retention of [e] before voiceless consonants, even in accented syllables—for example, [et], [ep], and [ek].

DRILL

Write several lines of the [e] symbol, saying it aloud and concentrating on the muscular movements involved as you write it. To write this symbol with the greatest economy of effort, begin the horizontal line by proceeding from left to right and, without lifting the pencil, abruptly begin a circular counterclockwise movement which intersects the left end of the horizontal line, and continues until approximately seven eighths of a circle is completed. Since this phonetic symbol is identical to the lower-case printed alphabetical symbol *e*, you will need to be especially careful to associate the correct sound with this particular symbol:

_____

_____

_____

_____

EXERCISE 16

Transcribe the following words:

1. craze _____		17. flail _____	
2. train _____		18. glades _____	
3. drape _____		19. slave _____	
4. blaze _____		20. display _____	
5. plate _____		21. crepe _____	
6. praise _____		22. drains _____	
7. preys _____		23. disgrace _____	
8. prays _____		24. trade _____	
9. scales _____		25. grade _____	
10. phrase _____		26. greyed _____	
11. frays _____		27. Spain _____	
12. snake _____		28. stale _____	
13. sprayed _____		29. swain _____	
14. straight _____		30. quail _____	
15. strait _____		31. brake _____	
16. clay _____		32. name _____	

EXERCISE 16: DISCUSSION

Look over your transcriptions for Exercise 16. You should have three identical word pairs, plus one group of three words which are sounded – and hence transcribed – identically. If you do not, you have been thinking of the spelling, not the sound of these words. Recheck your work until you find your errors.

EXERCISE 17

Underline the words in the following list which contain the sound [e]:

laid   said   suede   display   fate

grate   great   afraid   paid   aisle

evade   gauge   caught   guard   assuage

dame   daily   feign   deign

EXERCISE 17: DISCUSSION

Only four words will not be underlined if the exercise has been completed correctly.

DRILL

Read aloud the following word list as rapidly as you can:

[fɪt   fit   fet   pit   pɪt   pet   mɪd   mid   med
 til   tel   tɪl   sɪl   sel   sil   wik   wɪk   wek
 kɪl   kel   kil   lek   lik   lɪk]

EXERCISE 18

Transcribe the following words:

1. rainy _____   8. indeed _____

2. relief _____   9. tasty _____

3. evade _____   10. inane _____

4. ingrate _____   11. zany _____

5. Indies _____   12. liquid _____

6. braced _____   13. create _____

7. railway _____   14. lady _____

The vowel sound in the words *debt, ten,* and *red* is written in phonetics as [ɛ]. This phonetic symbol is called the *epsilon* and represents the first sound heard in our pronunciation of that Greek word. In making this sound the tongue is retracted more and humped slightly less than for the sound [e]. The mandible (lower jawbone) is lowered slightly more than for the [e]. The lips are in a relaxed, neutral position. This is a mid-front, lax, unround sound.

DRILL

Write the [ɛ] symbol twenty-five times, sounding it aloud as you do so. As you make each half circle, simultaneously associate the symbol with both the correct sound and the muscular movements necessary to draw and say it:

_____

_____

EXERCISE 19

Transcribe the following words:

1. wreck _____	10. hens _____	19. pick _____
2. lent _____	11. fence _____	20. peak _____
3. quest _____	12. step _____	21. peek _____
4. fell _____	13. breast _____	22. tent _____
5. west _____	14. deaf _____	23. tint _____
6. get _____	15. melt _____	24. taint _____
7. bled _____	16. decks _____	25. dead _____
8. slept _____	17. eggs _____	26. deed _____
9. bells _____	18. peck _____	27. did _____

28. peep _____	33. lays _____	38. least _____
29. pep _____	34. less _____	39. levy _____
30. pip _____	35. list _____	40. levee _____
31. lees _____	36. laced _____	41. pensive _____
32. Liz _____	37. lest _____	42. entry _____

DRILL

Read aloud the following words as quickly as you can, articulating clearly and precisely:

[fiz fez fɪz   bɛst bist best   drimd drɛmpt

trɪmd trɛnd trend   wɪk wek wik   skrɪm skrim

krɛpt krɪpt krikt   triz trez   trest trɪst]

EXERCISE 20

Read aloud the following sound combinations, circling those which are *not* legitimate words:

[flem   flɛm   flɛk   flɪk   flek   flik   revd   rɪft

lɛgz   ligz   tiks   teks   tɛkst   tɪks   skif   sken

skɛn   skm   pɛn   pin   pen   pɪm   lɛnd]

EXERCISE 20: DISCUSSION

Three words should be circled.

EXERCISE 21

Read the following pairs of words, and check each pair which does not contain a vowel sound common to both words:

1. heifer, quest _____	3. lent, said _____
2. breath, feat _____	4. siege, sieve _____

5. sage, beige _____   8. wreath, breathe _____

6. wretched, belch _____   9. blessed, been _____

7. breathe, Phoebe _____   10. scent, sent _____

EXERCISE 21: DISCUSSION

Two or three pairs should be checked, depending on how you pronounce *been*.

We are about to begin a series of exercises entitled "Troublesome Words." Some professional and other well-educated people pronounce some of these words in ways considered unacceptable to others. In addition, you may hear variants of these words which no well-educated person would accept.

Because many substandard pronunciations result from stressing the wrong syllable, we will include stress marks in transcribing all words in this series. In phonetic transcription the syllable given primary stress is indicated by placing a small vertical line *before* the syllable *above* the line of writing. For syllables receiving secondary stress, a small vertical line is placed before the syllable but *below* the line of writing. For example, ['mɪlˌstrim]. More complete discussions of stress are to be found on pages 59-60 and in Chapter 9.

It is suggested that the student transcribe the words in this series as he thinks he pronounces them and then compare his transcriptions with those of his fellow students and with the phonetic dictionary and other dictionaries. For some students this series of exercises might also serve as a vocabulary builder, since no student should complete these exercises without learning the meanings of unfamiliar words.

This series of exercises could be viewed as a step toward *prescriptive* phonetics, rather than as a continuation of the *descriptive* approach which typifies most of this book. This seeming entry into the realm of "what *should be* said" is made with a certain amount of uneasiness. Pronunciations are simply reflected in dictionaries; no dictionary is designed to make you change your pronunciation. They are, of course, helpful as a guide to pronunciation in the case of unfamiliar words. Even then, however, you must recognize that dictionaries often reflect a compromise between the ideas of strong-minded members of a pronunciation committee. In addition, you should realize that pronunciations change with time, but there is an inevitable time lag in reflecting these changes (or compromises of committee members). Despite the problems involved in checking this type of material, this series should be of value to most students. The exercises are designed to sharpen your awareness of your own pronunciations and to stimulate your interest in discovering the most commonly accepted standard English pronunciations of these troublesome words.

EXERCISE 22: TROUBLESOME WORDS

Transcribe the following, including stress marks:

1. bier _____   3. deaf _____

2. cuisine _____   4. mien _____

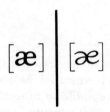

The next vowel sound to be considered is [æ] as in *hat*, *black*, and *grab*. This sound is often nasalized because of incomplete velopharyngeal closure (see p. 23). The symbol [~], which is called the *tilde*, is placed above phonetic symbols to indicate nasalization. A nasalized pronunciation of *hat* would be transcribed [hæ̃t]. Another modification frequently heard in the pronunciation of words requiring the [æ] sound is a drift toward [ɛ] or [e].

The [æ] sound demands a fairly wide mouth opening, with the tongue lying low in the mouth, both anteriorly and posteriorly. The downward movement of the mandible is greater than that for the sound [ɛ]. There are both lax and somewhat tense allophones of this phoneme. The [æ] is low-front and unround. This is the lowest front vowel of the vowel sounds regularly used throughout the United States. (See page 57 for the lower, but somewhat more centralized, vowel [a].)

The [æ] symbol is written in one uninterrupted motion. Beginning in the upper left-hand corner, draw a curving line down to the lower left-hand corner, continue the line up and across horizontally, rising to the upper right-hand corner, and then continue down through the symbol's center with a rounding curve to the lower right-hand corner. Perhaps it would help to think of the symbol as composed of two parts beginning with [ə] and continuing with [e], joined together and written in an uninterrupted stroke, rounding the angular corners on each half of the symbol. Thus, the symbols [ə e] when joined appear as [æ].

DRILL

Write the [æ] symbol twenty-five times, sounding it as you do so. Get the feel of your arm movements while writing and simultaneously associate the symbol with the sound and the muscular movements necessary to both draw and say it:

_____

_____

EXERCISE 23

Transcribe the following words:

1. vat _____

2. lack _____

3. camp _____

4. fan _____

5. transept _____

6. Travis _____

7. napkin _____

8. transcend _____

9. mandrake _____

10. malice _____

11. candy _____

12. laminate _____

13. tranquil _____

14. lax _____

15. man _____

16. nagged _____

17. sack _____

18. valve _____

19. lattice _____

20. massive _____

21. panic _____

22. traffic _____

23. sagged _____

24. vaccine _____

EXERCISE 24

Circle the words which do *not* contain the [æ] sound:

rapid	aesthetic	ascetic	ascertain	aboard
hearth	vanish	flair	vanilla	vantage
mañana	manacle	traduce	trachea	tractable

bear	arid	care	arrive	career
scarce	Saxony	guarantee	quaff	vacate
heirloom	vaccine	whereas	malign	malice
Malaysian	malaise			

EXERCISE 24: DISCUSSION

Count the number of words you have circled. Depending upon your dialectal background, you should have circled between thirteen and twenty words. This suggests that there are seven words in the list for which different pronunciations prevail in different sections of the country. These words are: *flair, bear, arid, care, scarce, guarantee,* and *heirloom.* Either [ɛ] or [æ] is acceptable in these words. Note that in these words the [ɛ] or [æ] appears in the stressed syllable and is followed by *r.* The use of [æ] or [ɛ] in words of this type appears to be a matter of geography and is not yet accurately plotted. The [æ] is more common along the east coast, while the [ɛ] is more frequently used inland—at least in the northern areas of this country.

DRILL

Read aloud the following word list as rapidly as you can:

[hæd hɛd hɪd hid hez hɪz hæz ræft rɛft

rɪft griv grev grænd grend drɪp drep sæp

sip sɪp vɛst væst men mæn mɛn min]

EXERCISE 25: TROUBLESOME WORDS

Transcribe the following, including stress marks:

1. calumny _____   6. prevalence _____

2. ecstasy _____   7. panacea _____

3. epitome _____   8. recreant _____

4. emeritus _____   9. savory _____

5. once _____   10. surfeit _____

11. taciturn _____   13. zealous _____

12. vehemence _____   14. piquant _____

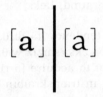

One other front, or more accurately front-central,[8] vowel sound in our language is made with a tongue position lower than that for the sound [æ]. This is the [a] sound used in eastern New England and parts of the South. Have your instructor produce this sound for you. Listen to it carefully; try to duplicate it. If you have difficulty try sliding from the sound [æ] to the sound [ɑ], as in *ah* or *psalm*. If you stop part-way between these sounds, you will be approximating the sound [a]. If you are still not satisfied that the acoustic result duplicates that of your instructor, try forcing the front of your tongue lower behind your lower gum line. Perhaps your class has a New Englander who uses this sound. Listen to him say it. If a recording of the phonetic alphabet is available, play it over and over, trying to duplicate this sound. Have your efforts checked by your instructor. Try using [a] in such words as *ask, aunt,* and *can't.* This practice is designed to sharpen your ability to identify sounds. You are not being asked to adopt this sound in your speech, if you don't already use it.

You will note that this is the lowest front (or front-central) vowel sound in the English language. The jaw is open farther than for any other vowel sound except the [ɑ] which doctors ask for when they wish to have us lower our tongues as far as possible so that they may peer down our throats. The [a] is low-front-central, lax and unround.

The symbol [a] is most easily written by beginning with the top curve and continuing downwards to form the "staff" of the symbol. Then the half circle is attached with a counterclockwise movement.

Chapter Summary

[ɪf ju] have studied [ðɪs tʃæptɚ kɛrfəlɪ, ju ʃʊd no] that vowel sounds can be described physiologically [ɪn tɝmz əv ðə ples (frʌnt, sɛntrəl, bæk)] and [haɪt (haɪ, mɪd, lo) əv tʌŋ hʌmpɪŋ], as well as [ɪn tɝmz əv mʌskjəlɚ tɛnʃən] and lip-rounding. [fɚ ðə frʌnt vauəlz, ðɪs ɪnfɚmeʃən] can be summarized as follows:

8. This sound has been variously judged to be a front, front-central, or central vowel. Thomas (1958, p. 115) defines it as "a low lax vowel formed with the tongue bunched in either the central or the front-central area."

[i] – [haɪ frʌnt, ʌnraʊnd, tɛns]

[ɪ] – [haɪ frʌnt, ʌnraʊnd, læks]

[e] – [mɪd frʌnt, ʌnraʊnd, tɛns]

[ɛ] – [mɪd frʌnt, ʌnraʊnd, læks]

[æ] – [lo frʌnt, ʌnraʊnd, (boθ læks n̩ tɛns æləfonz)]

[a] – [lo frʌnt sɛntrəl, ʌnraʊnd, læks]

[ju ɔlso] should be aware of the tendency [tə dɪfθɔŋaɪz] the tense sounds [i] and [ɛ]. [ɪf ju həv kəmplitɪd itʃ əv ðə ɛksɚsaɪzɪz wɪθ kɛr, vɝbəlaɪzɪŋ ðə saʊndz əz ju dɪd so, ju] should have begun to acquire [ə riznəbl̩ dɪgri əv skɪl ɪn hɪrɪŋ ðə frʌnt vauəl saʊndz ɪn wɝdz ən ɪn trænskraɪbɪŋ ðəm fənɔtɪklɪ. ju wɪl ɔlso həv startəd tə ʃarpən jur hɪrɪŋ] (and we hope your pronunciation) [əv trʌblsəm wɝdz].

chapter 4

THE CENTRAL VOWELS

The formation of [ɜ, ɝ, ɚ, ʌ, ə]
Syllabic stress

By this time you have learned the five front vowel sounds – [i, ɪ, e, ɛ] and [æ] – commonly used throughout the United States, as well as an additional sound – [a] – most common in the speech of Easterners. In this chapter we will study the sounds which are produced by humping the central part of the tongue. Although all languages utilize front and back vowels, certain languages, such as Spanish and Italian, do not contain these phonemes. These English phonemes, therefore, can cause special difficulties for some foreigners.

Basically, two groups of sounds are made by humping the central part of the tongue: the vocalic or vowelized *r*, as in *bird*, and the *uh* sound heard in such words as *up* and *luck*. These sounds are transcribed as [ɝ][1] and [ʌ], respectively Of the two sounds, the tongue is humped higher and the jaw opening is smalleɪ for the [ɝ]. The symbol [ɝ] is written like a number 3 with a caret attached near the top of the curve of the upper half of the symbol.

$$[\Lambda, \partial] \quad \Big| \quad [\Lambda, \partial]$$

You have undoubtedly noticed by now, particularly if your curiosity has led to the phonetic dictionary habit, that the [ʌ] sometimes appears to be represented by another symbol [ə]. Words such as *sofa* and *amend* have been transcribed as [sofə] and [əmɛnd]. Why not [sofʌ] and [ʌmɛnd]? Which symbol should be used depends on the stress given to the syllables within the word in question.

Say aloud any two-syllable word in our language. With very few exceptions, you will discover that one syllable receives greater stress than the other and

---

1. Readers interested in the controversy centering around the use of this symbol are referred to Albright (1958, pp. 59-61).

hence is perceived as more prominent. In most cases, this is the result of your making the stressed syllable a trifle louder and longer than the other. In addition, stress usually involves a pitch change; the stressed syllable is ordinarily pitched higher. Normally, variation of all three factors (pitch, loudness, and duration) occurs simultaneously. When the stressed syllable contains the *uh* sound, the symbol [ʌ] is used. When the same sound occurs in an unstressed syllable, it is transcribed as [ə].

The [ə] symbol is called the *schwa*, pronounced [ʃwɑ]. This is the sound of the vocalized pause frequently heard in hesitant speaking. It is also called the neutral vowel sound, because at certain times the [ə] is the acceptable pronunciation for the unstressed form of every vowel in the language. Since reduced stress almost always means a shortening of the duration of the syllable, there is insufficient time for the precise articulatory movements necessary to produce what we call tense vowels. Hence we produce such vowels as [ə] and [ɪ] in unstressed syllables. The [ʌ] and [ə] are lax, central,[2] unround vowel sounds.

The words *discus*, *Anna*, and *elevate* are transcribed [dɪskəs], [ænə] and [ɛləvet]. However, *discuss*, *culprit*, and *country* are transcribed [dɪskʌs], [kʌlprɪt] and [kʌntrɪ]. Note the clarity afforded by these two symbols when the same sound appears more than once in a word, as in [rʌmpəs] or [səpʌlkrəl]. The phonemes clearly indicate which syllable is stressed.

EXERCISE 26

List five more words which include both the stressed [ʌ] and the unstressed [ə] sounds:

_____

_____

When writing the symbol [ʌ], begin with a short rising straight line and conclude with a straight line returning to the line of writing. The [ə] symbol is begun with a clockwise movement, ending in a left-to-right horizontal line.

DRILL

Write two lines of these symbols, alternating the two. Associate each symbol with the correct sound and the muscular movements necessary to write it. As you alternate symbols, reflect the stress differences by saying the [ʌ] loudly and the [ə] softly:

_____

_____

---

2. For the use of this classification see the footnote on page 38.

EXERCISE 27

Write the following words in phonetics:

1. succeed _____
2. public _____
3. success _____
4. insult _____
5. sullen _____
6. musket _____
7. nutmeg _____

8. condemn _____
9. pundit _____
10. trumped _____
11. asleep _____
12. connect _____
13. lettuce _____
14. mullet _____

EXERCISE 28

Circle any of the following words which do not contain the [ʌ] or [ə] sound:

rough   rouge   wrong   wrung   rung

cover   covert   covet   hiccough   mulatto

fuss   fuse   funny   thumb

EXERCISE 28: DISCUSSION

If you have circled more or less than three words, recheck your work.

$$[ɝ, ɚ, ɜ] \mid [ɝ, ɚ, ɜ]$$

Just as there are two symbols to represent the *uh* sound, so are there two symbols for the vocalic *er* sound. This is the sound present in words such as *bird*, *hurt*, *return*, and *earned*. When this sound is emphasized, it is transcribed [ɝ], as in [bɝn], [ɝnd], and [hɝs]. This symbol is called the hooked reversed epsilon. When the sound is heard in an unstressed syllable, it is transcribed [ɚ], as in [lædɚ], [ɛntɚ], and [bɪdɚ]. This symbol is called the hooked schwa. Of the two central unround *er* sounds, [ɝ] is tense and [ɚ] is lax. The hook on each of the central *er* sounds indicates *r*-coloring, which is produced either by humping the central portion of the tongue higher in the mouth than for [ʌ], or by raising (or retroflexing) the tongue tip toward the alveolar ridge. In writing the hooked schwa, begin the same as with the schwa, but instead of finishing with a horizontal line, complete the symbol with a rising diagonal terminating in a little caret outside the circle, as follows: ɚ

An additional central vowel [ɜ], the reversed epsilon, is used in eastern New England, in the South, and by a certain percentage of the citizens of New York City. It is used in words requiring a stressed *er* sound by people who do not use the *r*-coloring associated with the sound [ɝ]. Those who use this sound usually use the [ə] in place of unstressed [ɚ] as well.

DRILL

Write two lines of the *r*-colored symbols, alternating one with the other, and associating the symbol with the correct sound and the muscular movements necessary to write them. As you alternate symbols, reflect the stress differences by saying the [ɝ] loudly and the [ɚ] softly:

_____

_____

EXERCISE 29

Circle all of the following words containing *er* sounds which would be transcribed as [ɝ]:

concern	concur	colonel	governor	candor
turf	Easter	burgher	turkey	tenor
verse	disburse	turgid	platter	

EXERCISE 29: DISCUSSION

Nine words should have been circled. The word *burgher* contains both stressed and unstressed *er* sounds.

EXERCISE 30

Transcribe phonetically all the words in the previous exercise which contain [ɚ]:

_____

_____

EXERCISE 31

Transcribe the following words:

1. desert _____	9. irks _____
2. dessert _____	10. renter _____
3. curtain _____	11. service _____
4. murder _____	12. perplex _____
5. mutter _____	13. urban _____
6. muddy _____	14. suburban _____
7. bloody _____	15. converse _____ *(verb)*
8. decanter _____	16. converse _____ *(adjective)*

You are now beginning to understand the use of different symbols for similar sounds receiving different degrees of stress. The question arises, however, as to which symbol should be used in a one-syllable word. The following rule can be followed *for the time being:* All one-syllable words will be transcribed with the accented symbol, except for the small filler words such as *of, the* and *a*. These exceptions are transcribed with the schwa as [əv], [ðə], and [ə]. This principle will be clarified later, after you have acquired more skill in transcribing individual words phonetically.

EXERCISE 32

Many of the following words are incorrectly transcribed. Write the correct transcription after each incorrect one:

1. circus   [sɚkʌs] _____

2. citron   [sɪtrən] _____

3. deserve   [dɪzɚv] _____

4. interlace   [ɪntɚles] _____

5. cellar   [sɛlɚ] _____

6. inward   [ɪnwɝd] _____

7. quirk   [kwɝk] _____

8. submersed   [səbmɚst] _____

9. urban   [ɝbən] _____

10. wizard   [wɪzɚd] _____

11. disrupt   [dɪsrəpt] _____

12. gust   [gəst] _____

13. matter   [mætɝ] _____

14. mister   [mɪstɝ] _____

15. pumice   [pʌmɪs] _____

16. purse   [pɝs] _____

EXERCISE 32: DISCUSSION

You should have corrected half of the above words. Numbers 1, 3, 6, 8, and 11 through 14 were incorrectly transcribed.

[tʃæptɚ sʌmərɪ]

[θɝo, kɛrfəl stʌdɪ əv ðɪs tʃæptɚ ʃud əv ɪmpruvd jur əbɪlətɪ tə rɛkəgnaɪz ðɪ ʌnraund sɛntrəl vauəl saundz ɝ, ɚ, ɚ, ʌ, n̩d ə. ɪn ədɪʃən tə bɪgɪnɪŋ tə trænskraɪb ðɪz saundz, ju ʃud ɔlso həv lɝnd hau ðe ɚ prədust, ənd ðɛr:ɪleʃən tə sɪlæbɪk strɛs].

chapter 5

ADDITIONAL CONSONANT SOUNDS

The syllabic consonants [l̩, m̩, n̩]
Homorganic consonants
The formation of [ŋ, θ, ð, ʃ, ʒ, tʃ, dʒ, hw, ʍ, j]
Digraphs
Troublesome words

Before you start using some of the more unusual-looking consonant sound symbols, let us look at a modification of three of the consonant symbols we have been using. Exercise 33 will help us pinpoint the difference.

$$[\, l̩, \, m̩, \, n̩ \,] \quad [\, l̩, \, m̩, \, n̩ \,]$$

EXERCISE 33

Transcribe the following:

1. apple _____

2. girdle _____

3. fiddle _____

4. Britain _____

5. treason _____

6. fasten _____

7. surrealism _____

8. swizzle _____

9. sadden _____

10. saddle _____

11. eaten _____

12. little _____

EXERCISE 33: DISCUSSION

Did the word endings in this exercise raise any transcription problems? Did you precede all final consonants with the schwa sound [ə]? Did you use any other vowels before any of the final consonants? Were you tempted to use no vowel before the final consonant in any of the words? If not, try saying these words fairly rapidly in sentences. Would you now be tempted to omit the vowel sound in any of the final syllables?

In words such as those in Exercise 33, most of us omit the vowel sound in the final syllable when speaking with any reasonable degree of speed. However, as you will recall from Chapter 1, we have insisted that a syllable must contain a vowel sound or vowel substitute.

The sounds [l], [m], and [n] can act as vowel substitutes. If we proceed from the [p] to the [l] sound in the word *apple* without uttering an identifiable vowel sound, we say that the [l] is a *syllabic consonant*. By this we mean that the [l] takes the place of a vowel, creating another syllable in the word without the presence of a true vowel sound. To show that the phoneme is performing this function, we place under it a dot, called the *syllabic mark*.[1] Word transcription using this mark would appear as follows: [æpl̩], [trizn̩], [sərɪəlɪzm̩].

Syllabic consonants occur most frequently when two successive, easily linked consonants in adjacent syllables are *homorganic*. Homorganic consonants are those which have identical places of articulation. The [t], [d], [l], and [n] sounds are homorganic in that their production requires the placing of the tongue tip on the alveolar ridge. Thus, we can move from the articulation of the [t] in *kitten* to the [n] by simply lowering the velum. Similarly, in pronouncing *rattle*, we can progress from the [t] to the [l] by simply lowering the sides of the tongue. In both words the tongue tip remains on the alveolar ridge. Since the tongue does not approximate the position for any vowel sound in executing the movements required for such combinations, a vowel sound is not heard and the final consonant is a *syllabic* (see G. I.). Were the tongue tip to leave the alveolar ridge, some type of intervening vowel sound – probably [ə] – would be heard, and the final sound would not be a syllabic.

In the first example of a syllabic given above – the [l̩] in the word *apple* – the two consonants were not homorganic. Despite the difference in the places of articulation, this sequence of consonants can be said without an intervening vowel sound by placing the tongue in position for [l] before exploding the [p].

It is possible to close off the air stream with the [n] tongue position so rapidly after the [z] sound in *reason* that the formation of a vowel sound between [z] and [n] is prevented, resulting in the pronunciation [rizn̩]. Of course this word can also be pronounced with an intervening vowel sound, as [rizən].

The best way to determine whether or not a consonant is syllabic is to listen very carefully. If you do not hear a vowel sound in a given syllable, you have a syllabic consonant. In Exercise 33, all of the syllabic consonants appeared at the ends of words. They are also found within words, though not as frequently.

---

1. Some phoneticians use a small vertical line or a small circle (Trager and Smith) as the syllabic mark. In this book we will use the dot.

EXERCISE 34

Transcribe each of the following with a syllabic consonant:

1. effervescence _____

2. fascinate   _____

3. rattletrap   _____

4. hedonist   _____

5. vacillate   _____

EXERCISE 35: TROUBLESOME WORDS

Transcribe the following, including stress marks:

1. escape _____   7. medieval _____

2. grievous _____   8. victuals _____

3. irrelevant _____   9. schism _____

4. bacchanal _____   10. clandestine _____

5. cavalry _____   11. legate _____

6. latent _____   12. prelate _____

In the chapter summaries you have been reading some transcribed words using the symbol [ŋ]. This is the sound appearing after the vowel sound in words such as *sang, swing, wrong,* and *ring.* It is made by bringing the back of the tongue and the velum (soft palate) together, opening the velopharyngeal port, and vibrating the vocal folds. By bringing the tongue and velum together so that only the oral cavity is closed off, you can resonate the vocalized air in the nasal cavities and expel it through the nostrils. Hence [ŋ] is a voiced, velar, nasal sound. To write the symbol [ŋ], simply add the tail of a *g* to the [n].

DRILL

Write two lines of alternate [n] and [ŋ] sounds, saying them slowly as you write them, and concentrating on where the tongue closes off the oral exit:

_____

_____

You will note that for the [n] sound, the tongue closes off the oral cavity further forward in the mouth. The air is trapped by placing the front of the tongue on the inner surface of the alveolar ridge (upper gum ridge), rather than on the velum as for the [ŋ]. The sides of the tongue are against the molars. The difference in sound between [n] and [ŋ] is due to the use of the mouth as a resonator in the production of the [n].

EXERCISE 36

Transcribe the following words in phonetics:

1. fan _____

2. fang _____

3. bing _____

4. been _____

5. bean _____

6. pin _____

7. ping _____

8. done _____

9. dung _____

10. ton _____

11. tongue _____

12. blank _____

13. spunk _____

14. fungus _____

15. hank _____

16. tanker _____

17. finger _____

18. anger _____

19. cinder _____

20. sphincter _____

21. Ingrid _____

22. ingress _____

23. Hemingway _____

24. sanguine _____

EXERCISE 36: DISCUSSION

Do not read the next paragraph until you have transcribed the words in Exercise 36. Now check your work. The first two words are [fæn] and [fæŋ]. But what happened in the next three words? Do you have an [i] in *bing*? If so, you are not sounding the word as most native Americans would. This word is usually pronounced [bɪŋ]. A good rule to remember is that we rarely use the sound [i] immediately before [ŋ]. You probably have no questions about the word *been*. However, were you to compare your answer with that of someone else in your phonetics class, you might discover a different version. This word is pronounced either [bɪn] or [bɛn]. It is also pronounced [bin] by many Britishers and Canadians. Make listening for the word *been* a goal for today. You may be quite surprised at how many people say this word differently than you do. *Bean* should be transcribed [bin].

The next six words in the above exercise should be transcribed [pɪn, pɪŋ, dʌn, dʌŋ, tʌn, tʌŋ]. Be sure you did not transcribe the next word as [blænk]. If you did, say the first four sounds, then try putting on a [k] without changing the sound of the preceding [n]. When *ng* or *nk* terminates a syllable, [ŋ] occurs. Can you tell why? For the answer to this, think in terms of how these sounds are produced.

The next five words should be transcribed [spʌŋk, fʌŋgəs, hæŋk, tæŋkɚ, fɪŋgɚ]. Notice that in some of these words the [ŋ] is followed by a [g]; in others it is not. If a [g] is heard, it must be transcribed.

The last seven words should be transcribed [æŋgɚ, sɪndɚ, sfɪŋktɚ, ɪŋgrɪd, ɪŋgrɛs, hɛmɪŋwe, sæŋgwɪn]. Be sure you understand all of your errors; sound out several times any words which you transcribed incorrectly.

You have now been exposed to some of the more troublesome [ŋ] combinations. This sound might seem quite simple to detect after all. In actual speech, however, the [ŋ] is one of the most carelessly pronounced consonant sounds in our language. How many times do we hear [hiz pleɪən tɛnɪs] or [hiz goən aut]? Some students of phonetics begin to take the "so what?" attitude toward this kind of sloppy diction: "After all, everyone knows what you're sayin'." Perhaps this is true, but teachers of speech and English have steadfastly resisted the trend toward changing final [ŋ] to [n] in participles. Thus, although this careless use of [n] for [ŋ] does not impair understanding, it is still considered substandard. Also substandard is the use of a final [n] in such words as *nothing* and *something*.[2]

According to Kenyon and Knott, [ŋ] is sometimes acceptable as a syllabic immediately following the velar [k], as in *I can go* [aɪkŋgo] and *bag and baggage*

2. You could expect Spanish-speaking people to have difficulty pronouncing final-*ng* words correctly, since the Spanish language does not contain the phoneme /ŋ/. However, immediately preceding [k] and [g], Spaniards do produce an [ŋ] allophone of the /n/ phoneme, as in "blanco."

[bægŋbægɪdʒ]. Since [ŋ] is *always* syllabic after a consonant, it is not necessary to include the syllabic mark.

$$[\theta, ð] \quad | \quad [\Theta, ꝺ]$$

Two sounds frequently mispronounced are the *th* sounds. These sounds are produced in exactly the same manner except for the presence or absence of voicing. Both of these sounds are made with the velopharyngeal port closed. The tongue tip is placed lightly against the upper front teeth (hence the designation *dental* sounds); the sides of the tongue touch the upper molars. The two *th* sounds can also be made interdentally – that is, with the tongue slightly protruded between the teeth. A column of air is forced between the frontal lingua-dental contact.

Words such as *thin, three,* and *thank* begin with [θ], the unvoiced *th,* called *theta* [θetə]. This sound also appears within and at the ends of words, as in *breathless, zither, uncouth,* and *bath.* In brief, [θ] is a voiceless, dental fricative. The symbol is written entirely above the line of writing and is a little less than twice the height of the vowel sound symbols. When voicing (vibration of the vocal folds) is added to this sound, the result is indicated by the symbol [ð], sometimes called the *crossed d.* The *crossed d* is a voiced, dental fricative. This sound initiates such words as *then, there,* and *those.* It also appears in other positions within a word, as in *rather, breathing, soothe,* and *bathe.* The symbol [ð] can be most efficiently written by starting at the top of the circle and going counterclockwise, rising for the tail, which is then crossed. The height of the completed symbol is a little less than twice that of the vowel sound symbols.

Many foreigners have trouble with the two *th* sounds because of the absence of these sounds in their native languages. This is true of Western European languages, with a few exceptions (notably, English, Spanish, and Danish). The substitution of [d] or [t] for the *th* sounds in words such as *these, those, them,* or *northeast* is one of the most obvious examples of substandard English pronunciation.

Speech correctionists frequently encounter the two *th* sounds, or at least approximations of them, as substitutions for the [s] and [z] sounds. This type of s-distortion is called a frontal lisp. Another common articulation problem of young children is the substitution of the [f] and [v] for the two *th* sounds. Many is the [mʌvɚ] who works to remove the [fʌm] from the [mauf].

Another type of articulation problem is the lateral lisp, which is phonetically transcribed as a voiceless *l* [l̥]. Instead of the breath stream being forced out of the front of the mouth for the [s] sound, the sides of the tongue are lowered to permit the air stream to escape laterally from the sides of the mouth.

DRILL

Practice writing three lines of the symbols for the *th* sounds, alternating the voiced and voiceless forms. Be sure to say the sound aloud while writing its symbol, concentrating on the various feedback stimuli which will help you establish the sound-symbol association:

_____

_____

_____

EXERCISE 37

Transcribe in phonetics:

1. heathen _____
2. myth _____
3. rather _____
4. eleventh _____
5. thirteenth _____
6. brother _____
7. length _____
8. theatrical _____
9. monthly _____
10. antithesis _____
11. wreath _____
12. threaten _____

13. thirsty _____
14. theory _____
15. Catholic _____
16. twelfth _____
17. earthen _____
18. thinking _____
19. featherweight _____
20. pathetic _____
21. absinthe _____
22. earthward _____
23. weathervane _____
24. Thanksgiving _____

EXERCISE 38

Circle the words containing the voiced *th*, or [ð] sound:

thorn	though	this	thistle	thither
through	lethal	forthwith	forsooth	farthing
brothel	brotherhood	phthisis	there	either
theory	thine	thence	oaths	Cathay
bismuth	calisthenics			

EXERCISE 38: DISCUSSION

Did you circle ten words? (*Oaths* was included in this total. It can, however, also be pronounced with the voiceless *th*.) *Forthwith* would boost the total to eleven if you pronounce its final sound as [ð].

$$[\int, \mathbf{3}] \,\Big|\, [\int, \mathbf{3}]$$

In making the [ʃ] (*sh*) sound, as in *she, fashion*, and *fish,* the sides of the tongue are raised and touch the inner surfaces of the upper molars. The unvocalized breath stream travels down a wide groove in the middle of the tongue, being directed toward the alveolar (gum) ridge. The passageway here is somewhat wider and the whole tongue is farther back in the mouth than is true for the [s] sound. The lips are usually slightly protruded. The resulting sound is classified as a voiceless fricative. Depending on how far forward the point of narrowest constriction lies, the sound is further classified as a palatal or palato-alveolar sound. Many individuals produce this sound with considerable lip rounding or puckering. The [ʃ] symbol should be drawn in a downward movement, with about three-quarters of the symbol appearing above the line of writing (about the height of the [l]), and approximately one-quarter below the line. The "stem" of the symbol should be relatively straight to prevent confusion with the more rounded [s] symbol.

Just as in the case of the two *th* sounds, the fricative [ʃ] has a voiced counterpart or *cognate*. When voicing is added to the sound [ʃ], the sound [ʒ] is produced. This sound appears in words of French derivation such as *beige, treasure,* and *collage* and in words of Latin and Greek origin, particularly those ending with the *-sion* spelling, such as *protrusion, confusion,* and *illusion.* In writing the symbol [ʒ], begin as for the [z], but in place of the bottom horizontal line make a circular tail extending almost as far below the line of writing as the other section extends above.

DRILL

Practice writing three lines of [ʃ] and [ʒ] sounds, alternating them. Be sure to say the sound aloud while writing its symbol, concentrating on the various feedback stimuli which will help you establish the sound-symbol association:

_____

_____

_____

EXERCISE 39

A. Circle the words in the second column which are incorrectly transcribed:

1. commercial   [kəmɝʒəl]   _____

2. Shakespeare   [ʃekspɪr]   _____

3. unction   [ʌŋkʃən]   _____

4. vision   [vɪzən]   _____

5. leisure   [liʃɚ]   _____

6. production   [prodʌktʃən]   _____

7. inertia   [mɝʒə]   _____

8. tension   [tɛnsən]   _____

9. heritage   [hɛrətɪʒ]   _____

10. countercharge   [kaʊntɚtʃɑrdʒ]   _____

11. decision   [dɪsɪʃən]   _____

12. bosom   [bʊzəm]   _____

13. chair   [ʃɛr]   _____

14. amnesia   [æmniʒɪə]   _____

15. English   [ɪŋglɪʃ]   _____

B. Transcribe correctly in the third column those words which are incorrectly transcribed in the second column above. When you have completed this correction, you will have changed all the words except numbers 2, 3, 10, 12, 14, and 15.

EXERCISE 40: TROUBLESOME WORDS

Transcribe the following, including stress marks:

1. meringue _____   6. chivalrous _____

2. malinger _____   7. defamation _____

3. precinct _____   8. perspiration _____

4. labyrinth _____   9. satiate _____

5. beige _____   10. vitiate _____

$$[t\int, d\check{z}] \mid [t\int, d\mathfrak{z}]$$

Exercise 39 used two consonant sound combinations which have been mentioned earlier in this text but not discussed. These are the [tʃ] and [dʒ] sounds. As in the case of the [θ] – [ð] and [ʃ] – [ʒ] pairs, these sounds are distinguished from one another by the presence or absence of voicing. Both [tʃ] and [dʒ] are composed of two separate consonant sounds rapidly succeeding each other. However, these particular combinations of plosive and fricative, unlike other combinations such as [ts] in *hats*, function linguistically in our language as one phoneme. The [t] and [s] in *hats* are functionally divisible or separable – in other words, *hats* can be reduced to *hat* without a recognized change of meaning (except, of course, for the change from plural to singular). This is not true for the [t] and [ʃ] in *hatch* [hætʃ] and *hatchet* [hætʃət]. The following word pairs show the contrast between the final sound complexes in terms of *separability*:

birch, Bert's   [bɝtʃ], [bɝts]

witch, wits   [wɪtʃ], [wɪts]

rage, raids   [redʒ], [redz]

budge, buds   [bʌdʒ], [bʌdz]

In these examples, the stops [t] and [d] in the second member of each pair are separable from the following [s] or [z] sound. The components of [tʃ] and of [dʒ], however, are not separable when either of these combinations occurs in a single syllable, and both [tʃ] and [dʒ] are therefore considered to be single phonemes.

The [tʃ] sound is made exactly as the [ʃ] with a [t] initiation of that sound. The resulting combined sound has phonemic significance and will therefore be treated — like each of the diphthongs — as one sound complex. In this book the [tʃ] and [dʒ] will each be referred to as one *sound*, despite the inaccuracy of this description. Such two-symbol combinations representing single sounds are called *digraphs*. In terms of manner of production, the [tʃ] and [dʒ], which contain both plosive and fricative elements, are designated *affricates*. Since these are the only two such combinations in our language which have phonemic significance, the list of *affricates* will be limited to [tʃ] and [dʒ].

In the light of the preceding explanation, when we say that [dʒ] is the voiced cognate of [tʃ], we have in essence described how that phoneme is produced. For your own clarification, use the space below to write a complete description of how the [dʒ] sound is produced:

_____

_____

_____

_____

EXERCISE 41: TROUBLESOME WORDS

Transcribe the following, including stress marks:

1. cache _____

2. chaff _____

3. chasm _____

4. chic _____

5. chicanery _____

6. gibbet _____

7. indigenous _____

8. mischievous _____

9. nuptials _____

10. chaise _____

11. picture _____

12. tragedian _____

EXERCISE 42

Transcribe the following:

1. pageant _____   7. heritage _____

2. charity _____   8. twinges _____

3. chasten _____   9. wheelchair _____

4. visage _____   10. chimpanzee _____

5. cherish _____   11. divulge _____

6. plagiarism _____   12. sanction _____

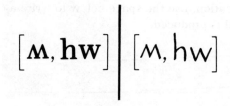

In Exercise 42, with what symbol did you begin number 9? Do you say the word *wheel* exactly the same as *we'll*? Is the word *which* pronounced the same as *witch*? These words raise the question of an interesting distinction in our language which is falling into disuse. The traditionalist would still insist that the words *where, when, why,* and *wheel* do not begin with the same sound as *wear*. He would transcribe those words as [hwɛr, hwɛn, hwaɪ, hwil] or as [ʍɛr, ʍɛn, ʍaɪ, ʍil]. According to Wise (1957, p. 145), the sound represented by the symbol [ʍ], or inverted *w*, includes no [h] sound; the friction is in the mouth, not in the glottis.

The [hw] sound is made by initiating the [w] sound with the [h] sound. The [w] sound is a voiced movement from the position required for the vowel [u], as in the word *too*, to whatever position is required by the following vowel sound. The [hw] sound, therefore, is a glide and is a combination of voiceless and voiced sounds. In [ʍ], however, the sounds [h] and [w] lose their original identities and blend into a voiceless fricative – the friction being oral rather than glottal (Kenyon, 1950, p. 42).

Because the distinction between [w]-[ʍ] and [w]-[hw] is ignored today in the speech of so many prominent people, many speech correctionists no longer are concerned with the matter and do not bother about the [ʍ] or [hw] sound in their therapy. Whether or not the distinction is taught in language arts courses for future elementary school teachers depends on the philosophy of the particular teacher or school of education. One of the more obvious reasons for the trend of defection from use of the [hw] sound is that it makes a distinctive difference in so few words in our language. Since the distinction between [hw] and [ʍ] is not phonemic in English, the more familiar symbolization [hw] will be used in this book to refer to both of these sounds.

EXERCISE 43

Observing the distinction between [w] and [hw], transcribe the following:

1. wonder _____ 6. whimsical _____

2. welt _____ 7. wear _____

3. whelp _____ 8. where _____

4. whirl _____ 9. pinwheel _____

5. dissuade _____ 10. waited _____

EXERCISE 43: DISCUSSION

If you check your phonetic dictionary, you will find that numbers 3, 4, 6, 8, and 9 of the preceding exercise are transcribed with the [hw] sound.

One more sound will complete our discussion of the consonant sounds normally used in spoken English. The remaining consonant sound is that which initiates the word *yes*. Without this initial sound, the word would be sounded [εs], like the name of the alphabet letter preceding *t*. The sound heard at the beginning of the word *yes* is represented by the phonetic symbol [j]. This symbol should not be confused with the letter *j* or the [dʒ] sound most frequently associated with that spelling. Instead, the phonetic symbol [j] is used to designate the sound beginning such words as *yes, year, Yale, union, use,* and *Utah*.

This sound is a voiced movement which begins from the position required for the sound [i], with the tongue blade approaching the anterior hard palate, and terminates in the position required for the following vowel sounds. You can see that because of its nature this sound must glide into a vowel sound. The sound, accordingly, is a voiced, palatal glide. For the start of this sound, the tongue tip usually remains behind the lower front teeth, while the front of the tongue is raised. This sound (even more than most) is partly determined by the following vowel sound.

As in the case of the [w] sound, the [j] is sometimes designated a *semivowel* to indicate its changing vowellike aspects. Like [w], [j] is sometimes unvoiced. Discussion and examples of this nonvoicing will be delayed until the presentation of the vowel [u] in the following chapter. In writing the [j] symbol, the stem of the symbol begins at the level of the imaginary "vowel line", with about one-third of the stem extending below the line of writing.

EXERCISE 44

Transcribe the following:

1. east _____   11. lung _____

2. yeast _____   12. young _____

3. least _____   13. jet _____

4. hams _____   14. yet _____

5. yams _____   15. let _____

6. lambs _____   16. yesterday _____

7. ail _____   17. Yank _____

8. hail _____   18. Spaniard _____

9. Yale _____   19. semiyearly _____

10. wail _____   20. brilliant _____

EXERCISE 45

You should now have command of enough phonetic symbols to transcribe into phonetics the pronunciation of the following fourteen of the fifty United States:

1. Alabama _____   4. Delaware _____

2. Alaska _____   5. Indiana _____

3. Connecticut _____   6. Kansas _____

7. Kentucky _____   11. Nebraska _____

8. Maine _____   12. Nevada _____

9. Maryland _____   13. Tennessee _____

10. Mississippi _____   14. Texas _____

[tʃæptɚ sʌməri]

[tə sʌmərɑɪz ðə fɔrmeʃən əv ɔl ðə kansənənt saʊndz jutḷɑɪzd ɪn ɪŋglɪʃ, wi kən:aʊ æd ðə 'fonɪmz stʌdɪd ɪn ðɪs tʃæptɚ tə ðoz əv tʃæptɚ tu ṇd kəmplit ðə tʃɑrt hwɪtʃ əpɪrd ɪn parʃəl fɔrm an pedʒ θɝtɪfɑɪv. əgɛn, lɑɪk ðæt (ɪnkəmplit) tʃɑrt əv kansənənt saʊnd fɔrmeʃən, ðɪs tʃɑrt wɪl ɪndəket ðə ples əv artɪkjələʃən bɑɪ ðə ro hɛdɪŋz, ənd ðə mænɚ əv prədʌkʃən bɑɪ ðə kaləm hɛdɪŋz. wɪðɪn itʃ pɛrɪŋ əv stap, frɪkətɪv, ənd æfrɪkɪt sɪmbḷz, ðə fɝst mɛmbɚ əv ðə pɛr ɪz ʌnvɔɪst, ðə sɛkənd ɪz vɔɪst. ðɪ ʌnpɛrd h ɪz vɔɪsləs. ɪn ðə rɪmenɪŋ kaləmz, ðə lætərəl ənd ɔl əv ðə nezḷz ən glɑɪdz ɚ vɔɪst, wɪð:ɪ ɪksɛpʃən əv hw hwɪtʃ ɪz ə kambənəʃən əv ðɪ ʌnvɔɪst h ən ðə vɔɪst w. ɪt ʃʊd bɪ rɪmɛmbɚd, əv kɔrs, ðət ðə æləfon ʍ ɪz ʌnvɔɪst.]

[əmɛrəkən ɪŋglɪʃ kansənənt saʊndz

	stap	frɪkətɪv	nezḷ	lætərəl	glɑɪd	æfrɪkɪt
bɑɪlebɪəl	p b		m		w hw	
lebɪodɛntḷ		f v				
(lɪŋgwə)dɛntḷ		θ ð				
(lɪŋgwə)ælviələ	t d	s z	n	l	l r	
(lɪŋgwə)pæləto ælviələ		ʃ ʒ				tʃ dʒ
(lɪŋgwə)pælətḷ		ʃ ʒ			j r	tʃ dʒ
(lɪŋgwə)viləˈ	k g		ŋ			
glatḷ		h]				

chapter 6

THE BACK VOWELS

The formation of [u, ʊ, o, ɔ, ɑ, ɒ]
Diphthongs [ʊu] and [oʊ]
Troublesome words

So far we have considered the *front* and *central* vowels. We will now consider the *back* vowels [u, ʊ, o, ɔ, ɑ, ɒ] and certain allophonic variations of these vowels. These sounds are called back vowels because they are made with the back of the tongue humped toward the back of the mouth.

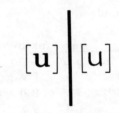

The vowel sound produced with the highest back tongue humping is the sound [u], as in the words *food, lose,* and *spoon.* This sound is made with the lips puckered and relatively tense and with the teeth slightly parted. It is a high-back, tense sound. The lips are strongly rounded.

DRILL

A. Write two lines of the symbol [u], saying it aloud and getting the muscle sense of its general shape as you say and write it:

B. Practice writing two lines of symbols, alternating the [u] with the [i]. As you say and write the symbols, concentrate on the kinesthetic feedback from the alternately puckered and retracted lips and alternate back and front tongue humping:

_____

_____

EXERCISE 46

Circle the words in the following list which contain the sound [u]:

snout	snoot	group	grouse	Peru
dud	dude	allude	aloof	up
user	usher	dumb	tomb	tome
dune	dunce	drew	Druid	drug
ducal	duchy	Magoo	preclude	menu
intrude	exude	exult	plume	plum
plumage	plump	Pluto		

EXERCISE 46: DISCUSSION

Did you circle twenty words? If not, review your work. If you still do not locate twenty words containing the sound [u], check with your classmates, your dictionary, or your teacher.

EXERCISE 47

Transcribe the following:

1. soothed _____ 5. crusade _____

2. uncouth _____ 6. papoose _____

3. illusion _____ 7. cruet _____

4. school _____ 8. kangaroo _____

9. proof _____   15. canoe _____

10. crudity _____   16. crucifix _____

11. groove _____   17. seclusion _____

12. rouge _____   18. thumbscrew _____

13. soufflé _____   19. breadfruit _____

14. suet _____   20. include _____

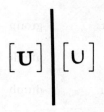

A sound somewhat similar to [u] is [ʊ][1], as in *foot, hook,* and *took.* This sound is made with a slightly lower tongue humping than that used for the sound [u], and with less puckering of the lips and significantly less tension of the lip muscles. Thus, it is a high-back, lax, rounded vowel sound. The [ʊ] is produced with a jaw opening only slightly larger than that demanded for [u]. This sound can be contrasted with the [u] sound in such word pairs as the following: *pull-pool, full-fool, could-cooed.*

Some phoneticians insist that two horizontal serifs be a part of this written symbol, so that it becomes [ʊ]. These may be omitted, however, *provided* that the bottom of the curve remains well rounded, so that the symbol will not be confused with [v], as in *vest.*

DRILL

A. Write the symbol [ʊ] twenty-five times, sounding it aloud as you do so. Associate the written symbol with the sound and the muscular movements necessary both to write and to say it:

_____

_____

_____

1. The 1947 revision of the IPA presents a different symbol for this sound, as well as for the sound represented in this text by the symbol [ɪ]. This book, in accord with the Kenyon and Knott phonetic dictionary, retains the older symbols [ʊ] and [ɪ] in preference to [ɷ] and [ɪ].

B. Practice simultaneously writing and saying two lines of phonetic symbols, alternating the [u] with the [ʊ] and concentrating on the different oral and aural feedback stimuli associated with each of these sounds. Note particularly the contrast in tension:

_____

_____

EXERCISE 48

Transcribe the following:

1. afoot _____   9. wood _____

2. supersede _____   10. look _____

3. underwood _____   11. root _____

4. bosom _____   12. roof _____

5. jurist _____   13. hoof _____

6. spool _____   14. soot _____

7. textbook _____   15. graduation _____

8. hookworm _____   16. priesthood _____

EXERCISE 48: DISCUSSION

In the preceding exercise the sound [ʊ] appeared in all of the words except numbers 2 and 6, which contained the sound [u]. Note that the fourth word might be pronounced with either [ʊ] or [u]. In words 11 through 14 the use of either [ʊ] or [u] is acceptable in America. Which pronunciation is used by the professional and other college-educated people in your community? Isn't it strange that, although these words can be pronounced with either the [u] or the [ʊ], we do not tolerate the alternative sound in the word *foot*? Perhaps you have also heard the word [puʃ] used to mean "to press forward." Is this pronunciation acceptable?

In the original reference to tense vowels in this book, we noted that such vowels tend to become diphthongized (see p. 46). The diphthongal [ʊu], as in *shoe*, is an allophone of the phoneme [u]. This allophone can be viewed as analogous to the [ɹi] allophone of the phoneme [i] in that it tends to be heard chiefly when serving as a stressed word ending. As in the case of the [ɹi] – [i] differentiations, this text will not require the allophonic distinction between [uu] and [u] since this difference is not a distinctive one in the English language. However, for foreigners whose language does not include both [u] and [ʊ] as different phonemes, the contrast in tension between the tense diphthongal [uu] and the short relaxed [ʊ] will help them differentiate more easily the [u] and [ʊ] sounds as used in American English.

EXERCISE 49

Circle the words in the following list which contain the sound [ʊ]:

cruise	cruet	crux	push	crook
stooge	stewed	could	cold	cooled
culled	wooed	wood	brook	platoon
good	consume	look	Luke	rule
dull	poultice	shoulder	should	nook

EXERCISE 49: DISCUSSION

Did you circle nine words? If not, review your work. If you still do not have nine [ʊ] words, check with your classmates, your dictionary, or your teacher.

EXERCISE 50

A. Transcribe the following:

1. rouge _____

2. crude _____

3. Sioux _____

4. gruesome _____

5. booze _____

6. exclude _____

7. bluebell _____

8. foot _____

9. clue _____

10. fully _____

11. wormwood _____   16. brook _____

12. aluminum _____   17. dachshund _____

13. peruse _____   18. Rudolf _____

14. use _____   19. gruesome _____
    (verb)

15. sleuth _____   20. tumescence _____

B. Underscore all of the above words which contain the [ʊ] sound.

EXERCISE 50: DISCUSSION

You should have underscored the following: 8, 10, 11, 16, and possibly 17. The Kenyon and Knott dictionary lists both [dɑkshʊnd] and [dæckshʌnd] for number 17. If you prefer to approximate the German pronunciation, you would substitute a [t] for the final [d] in the first version.

Take another look at your transcription of number 14 in this exercise. Have you transcribed this word as you would the word *ooze*? You have if you recorded [uz]. The first sound in *use* is not [u]. By comparing *ooze* and *use*, you should hear a [j] sound initiating the latter word.

EXERCISE 51

Transcribe the following:

1. centrifuge _____   9. repute _____

2. certitude _____   10. ridicule _____

3. diffusion _____   11. steward _____

4. magnitude _____   12. solicitude _____

5. newfangled _____   13. turpitude _____

6. New Year's _____   14. ubiquitous _____

7. constitute _____   15. union _____

8. petunia _____   16. vicissitude _____

EXERCISE 51: DISCUSSION

Of the sixteen words just transcribed, only numbers 14 and 15 *demand* the [j] before the [u] sound. Numbers 1, 3, 9, and 10 require either the combination [ju] or [ɪu], according to Kenyon and Knott. The remaining ten words can be acceptably pronounced with the [u] sound or the [ju] or [ɪu] combination.[2]

Now that we are acquainted with the [u] sound, we can consider the unvoiced [j] mentioned in the preceding chapter. When [j] appears in a stressed syllable, following a voiceless consonant—particularly the voiceless plosives—it is partially unvoiced, as in *impugn, Cuba,* and *tube*—[ɪmpju̥n], [kju̥bə], [tju̥b]. The reason for such unvoicing is that when the voiceless [p], [t], or [k] begins a stressed syllable, the strong force of breath (aspiration) is carried over, tending to prevent or obscure the voicing of the [j]. However, if the preceding voiceless [p], [t], or [k] functions in a [s] blend, as in [sp], [st], [sk], the stop is not aspirated and the [j] is voiced, as in *sputum, skewed,* or *stupid*—[spjutəm], [skjud], [stjupɪd].

EXERCISE 52: TROUBLESOME WORDS

Transcribe the following, including stress marks:

1. ludicrous _____   5. gesture _____

2. centrifugal _____   6. demur _____

3. February _____   7. cupola _____

4. penury _____   8. lugubrious _____

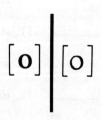

The next highest back vowel on the vowel chart (see Figure 6, p. 38) is the sound [o], as in *no, sew,* and *throw.* This sound is made with rounded lips and with the tongue humped slightly lower than for the sound [u]. It is a mid-back, rounded, tense vowel sound. In prolonging this tense sound, there is a tendency

---

[2]The use of [ju] varies considerably with respect to phonetic context and dialect areas (see Thomas, 1958, pp. 131-134).

for the tongue to rise somewhat, causing a glide towards the [ʊ] or [u] sounds. This creates a combination of vowel sounds called a *diphthong*.

The tendency to diphthongize the sound [o] varies throughout the United States. Indeed, the tendency varies within the speech of a given individual. However, as in the case of the sounds [i]-[ɪi], [e]-[eɪ], and [u]-[ʊu], there is no change of meaning in English words when the diphthong [oʊ] is substituted for the [o]. For this reason, and for the sake of convenience and speed in translation, we will use the one symbol [o] to designate any variation (including diphthongization) of [o]. Words in which Americans are least apt to diphthongize [o] are those in which another vowel follows immediately, such as *coagulate*, and those in which the syllable containing the [o] is not accented or emphasized, such as *rotogravure*.

When an actor tries to simulate the speech of a foreigner whose native language does not include the diphthong [oʊ], he will be more successful if he can minimize his native tendency to diphthongize the [o]. And the speech correctionist would do well to emphasize this diphthong in assisting foreigners to master spoken English.

EXERCISE 53

Transcribe the following:

1. widow _____   7. melodious _____

2. Halloween _____   8. hopeful _____

3. reproach _____   9. pueblo _____

4. sauté _____   10. theologian _____

5. pedagogy _____   11. production _____

6. zodiac _____   12. bemoan _____

EXERCISE 54: TROUBLESOME WORDS

Each of the following sentences contains a phonetic transcription of a common mispronunciation. In the space following the sentence, record the correct pronunciation, including stress marks, for the word in question:

1. All of the students received an [ɛpɪtom] of the work. (epitome) ____

_____

2. The earl spent the night in the local [geol]. (gaol) _____

3. My decision is [ɪrɪvokəbl̩]. (irrevocable) _____

4. Do you think the [wɪdɚ] will remarry? (widow) _____

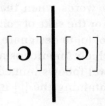

As the back humping of the tongue is progressively lowered while phonating, notice the progression from the sound [u] through [ʊ] to [o]. The next lowest back vowel is [ɔ] as in *law, awful,* and *caught.* This sound is made with a considerably wider jaw opening than that required for the [o]. It is a low-back, slightly tense, rounded vowel sound. Many phoneticians talk about the lips being rounded for this sound. Students who have trouble distinguishing between the low-back vowels and the middle vowel [ʌ] will probably best be able to form the sound of [ɔ] by thinking of the lip rounding as forming the oblong shape of the number 0 (zero). This can be done by keeping a fairly wide jaw opening and puckering the lips slightly.

DRILL

A. Write two lines of the symbol [ɔ], saying it aloud and acquiring a kinesthetic awareness of the movements used in writing the symbol:

_____

_____

B. Practice saying and writing two lines of symbols, alternating the [ɔ] with the [o], and concentrate on the difference in sound:

_____

_____

As you develop more acute listening habits, you will probably become aware of seeming inconsistencies in the use of [o] and [ɔ] before *r.* Historically, definite distinctions were made between such words as *horse* [hɔrs] and *hoarse* [hors], and between *morning* [mɔrnɪŋ] and *mourning* [mornɪŋ]. This distinction is gradually disappearing throughout most of the United States. The continuance of the distinction is strongest in the South and in the coastal regions of New England.

According to Wise (1957, p. 108), the following words are pronounced with either [o] or [ɔ] allophones: *ford, horde, sword, port, sport, forth, core, score, tore, coarse, hoarse, board, soar, roar, court, four, mourn, source, door, floor.*

EXERCISE 55

Transcribe the following:

1. gaunt _____   12. automotive _____

2. autumn _____   13. laudatory _____

3. laud _____   14. torture _____

4. taunt _____   15. walrus _____

5. falsetto _____   16. wherewithal _____

6. moths _____   17. gauntlet _____

7. brother-in-law _____   18. auditorium _____

8. flaunt _____   19. cobalt _____

9. Wichita _____   20. auditory _____

10. Falstaff _____   21. squall _____

11. orchestral _____   22. baldheaded _____

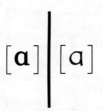

The lowest back vowel is the [ɑ], as in *calm* and *father,* as pronounced by most native Midwesterners. This vowel sound is made with the widest jaw opening of any of our vowel sounds. In contrast to the [ɔ] sound, [ɑ] is made with the corners of the lips retracted. Compare this difference visually by observing yourself in a mirror and kinesthetically by concentrating on the feel of the musculature while saying aloud the word pairs *pod* [pɑd]-*pawed* [pɔd] and *bawdy* [bɔdɪ]-*body* [bɑdɪ]. The [ɑ] sound can be described as low-back, lax, and unround.

DRILL

Write the [ɑ] symbol twenty-five times, sounding it aloud as you do so. Concentrate on associating the visible symbol with the sound and the muscular movements necessary both to write and to say it:

_____

_____

EXERCISE 56

Transcribe the following:

1. guitar _____   16. sergeant _____

2. harmful _____   17. conjugate _____

3. cargo _____   18. nonresistance _____

4. obligato _____   19. schoolyard _____

5. Oxydol _____   20. condescend _____

6. college _____   21. intoxicate _____

7. carillon _____   22. hippopotamus _____

8. despondent _____ 23. Slavic _____

9. Palmolive _____   24. Holland _____

10. potted _____   25. Yugoslavia _____

11. foolhardy _____ 26. Guatemala _____

12. autonomous _____ 27. Toscanini _____

13. hopscotch _____ 28. Antarctic _____

14. colossal _____   29. quatrain _____

15. helicopter _____ 30. hodgepodge _____

31. anonymous _____   36. cardiograph _____

32. propagation _____   37. epiglottis _____

33. lamasery _____   38. thrombosis _____

34. pathologist _____   39. toxicology _____

35. urology _____   40. physiologist _____

EXERCISE 57

Circle the words in the following list which do not contain the [ɑ] sound:

slotted	artful	heart	heard	beard
responsive	harness	Arnold	complication	complicity
Stalin	stale	stallion	stolid	stolen
store	star	stare	starve	statue
shot	shout	shoot	Bronx	bronze
bromide	brown	awful	insomnia	insouciant
southwest	soccer	socket	Socratic	

EXERCISE 57: DISCUSSION

Did you circle seventeen words? If not, review your work and check with your dictionary, classmates, or teacher.

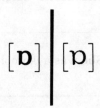

You may have noticed the qualification with respect to Midwestern pronunciation made in describing the sound [ɑ]. Many of the words normally pronounced with [ɑ] by native Midwesterners are pronounced with a different vowel sound by some Easterners and Britishers. These speakers use a sound roughly midway between the [ɑ] and the [ɔ]. The sound is represented by the symbol [ɒ]. This is the sound used in the pronunciation of *Boston* by many of that city's citizens. An approximation of this sound can be made by sliding back and forth between [ɑ] and [ɔ]. If you stop and prolong a sound partway between these sounds you will approximate the sound [ɒ], as in Eastern pronunciations of *odd* [ɒd] or *hot* [hɒt]. The sound is low-back and slightly rounded. Regional differences in the use of this sound are great; many of these are elaborated in Thomas (1958, pp. 117-122). If you are not familiar with this sound, be sure to listen closely to your instructor's pronunciation of it or to a recording of the phonetic alphabet if that is available.

EXERCISE 58: TROUBLESOME WORDS

Each of the following statements presents one or more pronunciations of the word preceding the statement. In the space provided, you are to indicate whether or not you agree with the transcription(s). If you agree with the pronunciation(s) given, record [j] for *yes*. If you disagree, record [n] for *no*. For each negative response, transcribe an acceptable pronunciation, including stress marks, in the space provided at the end of the sentence:

_____ blackguard   1. He's a [blækgɑrd]. _____

_____ caloric   2. What is the [kəlɔrɪk] content?

                        _____

_____ caramel   3. This type of candy is correctly called both

                        [kærəml̩] and [kɑrml̩]. _____

_____ chiropodist   4. Who is your [tʃɪrɑpədɪst]? _____

_____ cholera   5. The doctor diagnosed the disease as [kolərə].

                        _____

_____ comely   6. She was a [kɑməlɪ] woman.

                        _____

_____ comparable   7. These are not strictly [kəmpɛrəbl̩].

                        _____

_____ comptroller   8. Who is the [kɑmptrolɚ]? _____

_____ conduit 9. The linesman checked for breaks in the [kɑndɪt].

_____

_____ coupon 10. Send in fifty cents with your [kupɑn].

_____

_____ drama 11. [drɑmə] and [dræmə] are both acceptable pro-

nunciations. _____

_____ draught 12. The sign read "ale on [dræft]."

_____

_____ encore 13. The pianist played an [ɑnkɔr].

_____

_____ ennui 14. He was affected with [ɑnwi].

_____

_____ entree 15. Which [ɛntrɪ] did he select?

_____

_____ façade 16. It was an imposing [fəsɑd].

_____

_____ faux pas 17. He committed a [fo pɑs]. _____

_____ gendarme 18. He had been a [dʒɛndɑrm] for ten years.

_____

_____ geography 19. He is studying [dʒɑgəfɪ]. _____

_____ gondola 20. The [gɑndolə] carried them away.

_____

_____ guarantee 21. The mainspring carried a lifetime [gærənti].

_____

_____ halcyon   22. Those were [hælsɪən] days.

_____

_____ hiccough   23. He tried to suppress a [hɪkɔf].

_____

_____ ignoramus   24. They dismissed him as an [ɪgnəræməs].

_____

_____ jocund   25. They hired the [jɑkənd] man to play Santa Claus.

_____

_____ larynx   26. Voice is produced in the [lɑrnɪks].

_____

_____ longevity   27. Medicine has helped to increase [lɔŋgɛvətɪ].

_____

_____ novice   28. The player is strictly a [novɪs].

_____

_____ onerous   29. His duties were [onərəs] to him.

_____

_____ pharynx   30. His [fɑrnɪks] was inflamed.

_____

_____ probably   31. That is [prɑblɪ] your best choice.

_____

_____ quaffed   32. He [kwɑft] his ale quickly. _____

_____ quixotic   33. A [kwɪksɑtɪk] person would be a misfit among

pragmatists. _____

_____ resin   34. He bought some [rɛzn̩]. _____

_____ solace   35. The nurse was a constant source of [solɪs].

_____

_____ tarpaulin   36. The [tɑrpɔlɪn] was stretched over the hatch.

_____

_____ wash   37. Did you [wɔrʃ] the clothes? _____

[tʃæptɚ sʌmərɪ]

[ɪf ju əv kɛrfəlɪ stʌdɪd ðɪs tʃæptɚ ju ʃəd nau no hau ðə saundz u, ʊ, o, ɔ, ɑ, ənd ɒ ɚ prədust, ənd ju ʃud əv bɪɡʌn tu ətʃiv prəfɪʃənsɪ ɪn trænskraɪbɪŋ wɝdz kəntenɪŋ ðiz bæk vauəl saundz. ju ʃud ɔlso bɪ əwɛr əv ði əmɛrəkən tɛndənsɪ tə dɪfθɔŋaɪz boθ u n̩d o. ɪn ədɪʃən ju ʃud həv ɪmpruvd jɚ prənʌnsɪeʃən əv səm trʌblsəm wɝdz.]

chapter 7

THE DIPHTHONGS

The formation of [aɪ, aʊ, ɔɪ]
Fronting and retracting diphthongs
Centering diphthongs
The [ju] sound sequence
Troublesome words

If you will recall, we have already discussed four of the diphthongs used in American English. These were the [ɪi, eɪ, ʊu, oʊ] sounds which we agreed to represent with the simple symbols [i, e, u, o], since for these sounds the difference between the diphthong and the pure vowel is not a phonemic one in our language. However, the diphthongs [aɪ], [aʊ], and [ɔɪ], because of their phonemic functions, cannot be similarly abbreviated. Certainly no one will contend that [lɔn] has the same meaning as [lɔm].

$$[\mathbf{aɪ}] \mid [\mathbf{aɪ}]$$

By definition, a diphthong[1] is a continually changing blend of one vowel sound into another, occurring within the same syllable. The resulting blend functions as one phonemic entity. Hence, there is no syllable separation between these vowel sounds comprising a diphthong, as there is in the words *react* and *chaos*.

Just as the [eɪ] sound is the result of a rapid movement upward from the mid-front tongue humping for [e], so the [aɪ] sound results from a rapid glide of the tongue upward and forward from the [a] or [ɑ] position. (Figure 7 will help you visualize the tongue movements for the diphthongs.) Because the tongue rises toward the front vowel [ɪ], [aɪ]—like [eɪ]—is called a *fronting diphthong*. In

---

1. Etymologically the word *diphthong* suggests "two sounds." However, it would be more accurate to consider the vowel blend of a diphthong as the now stabilized *spreading* of one given vowel sound, not as the gliding together of two different vowel sounds.

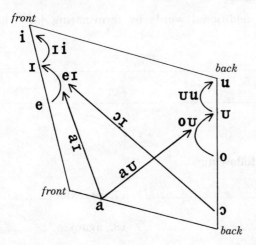

Fig. 7. Chart of the tongue movements for the diphthongs.

phonemic transcription we do not attempt to differentiate between the two start-ing positions [a] and [ɑ]. However, a reflection of these slight differences is noted in the allophonic notation used by some phoneticians. The [aɪ] symbol will be used exclusively in this book.

To repeat, the acoustic result which we will designate by the [aɪ] symbol is produced by an extremely rapid upward-forward movement of the tongue from either the low-front (or front-central) or lowest-back tongue position, while the vocal folds are vibrating. This is the complex vocalic blend we normally hear in the pronunciation of such words as *dime, right, quite, Nile,* and *guile.* In the South a common variation of this diphthong is created by sustaining the initial [a] element instead of raising the tongue toward the [ɪ] position, as in [daːm] and [raːt]. (See page 145 for a discussion of the mark of elongation [ː].)

DRILL

A. Write [aɪ] ten times, saying it aloud and concentrating on the sound and the muscular movements necessary to both write and say it:

_____

B. Practice writing this diphthong sound by transcribing at least ten words created by initiating [aɪ] with consonant sounds—for example, [baɪ] and [daɪ]. Be sure you say the words aloud while writing them:

_____

_____

_____

C. Create five additional words by terminating [aɪ] with consonant sounds:

_____

_____

EXERCISE 59

Transcribe the following:

1. Dwight _____   17. peroxide _____

2. Diana _____   18. agonize _____

3. ice _____   19. hijacker _____

4. Isaiah _____   20. nuclei _____

5. Einstein _____   21. exercise _____

6. idea _____   22. homogenize _____

7. nylon _____   23. knighthood _____

8. despite _____   24. womankind _____

9. isotope _____   25. genii _____

10. describe _____   26. macadamization _____

11. urbanite _____   27. bimonthly _____

12. desire _____   28. hieroglyphic _____

13. timer _____   29. psychometry _____

14. cross-eyed _____   30. bilingual _____

15. ramify _____   31. diabetes _____

16. nitrate _____   32. dioxide _____

EXERCISE 59: DISCUSSION

Did you use the diphthong [aɪ] in transcribing every one of the above words? The only possible exception is number 26, in which the fourth syllable can be the [ə] or the [aɪ]. Number 5 contains two [aɪ] sounds, while numbers 4 and 32 *may be* transcribed with two [aɪ] sounds each. Check your first vowel sounds in numbers 8, 10, and 12; they should all be the [ɪ]. Did you use a schwa [ə] in the second syllable of number 15? If so, you agree with Kenyon and Knott. Check number 16; the final vowel sound can be either [e] or [ɪ]. Did you begin number 20 with [nu] or [nju]? Both are acceptable.

EXERCISE 60: TROUBLESOME WORDS

Two alternative pronunciations are given for each of the following words. Circle the one which is least open to controversy:

1. calliope   a. [kəlaɪəpɪ]   b. [kælɪop]

2. demoniacal   a. [dimonɪækḷ]   b. [dimənaɪəkḷ]

3. facile   a. [fæsḷ]   b. [fesaɪl]

4. fiasco   a. [fɪæsko]   b. [faɪæsko]

5. heinous   a. [haməs]   b. [henəs]

6. ibis   a. [ɪbɪs]   b. [aɪbɪs]

7. indict   a. [ɪndɪkt]   b. [ɪndaɪt]

8. lichen   a. [laɪtʃən]   b. [laɪkən]

9. noblesse oblige   a. [noblɛsobliʒ]   b. [noblɛsoblaɪʤ]

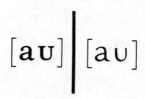

$$[aʊ] \mid [aʊ]$$

The diphthong [aʊ], like the diphthong [aɪ], begins with either the low-front (or front-central) [a] or the low-back [ɑ] tongue humping. Thomas (1958, p. 143) suggests that the frontal initiation is more common in eastern New England, New York City, the Middle Atlantic area, the South, and the Midland area (see Figure 1, page 7). This diphthong is the result of a quick movement of the tongue upward and backward toward the [u] or [ʊ] position, accompanied by voicing. The resulting sound is the vowel complex we normally produce in saying such words as *out*, *house*, and *stout*.

The rising tongue movement toward the back vowel [u] or [ʊ] accounts for the [aʊ] being classified as a *retracting diphthong*. The previously discussed [oʊ] would also be included in this classification. A common Southern variant of the [aʊ] is [æʊ].

DRILL

A. Write [aʊ] ten times, concentrating on the sound and the muscular movements necessary to both write and say it:

_____

_____

B. Transcribe ten words in which [aʊ] is initiated with consonant sounds. Be sure you sound aloud the words while writing them:

_____

_____

_____

C. Transcribe three additional words in which [aʊ] is terminated with consonant sounds:

_____

_____

EXERCISE 61

Transcribe the following:

1. output _____

2. breakdown _____

3. foundation _____

4. encounter _____

5. denounce _____

6. floundering _____

7. countercharge _____

8. outgrowth _____

9. chow mein _____

10. housewife _____

11. countersign _____

12. counterclockwise _____

EXERCISE 61: DISCUSSION

Which of the above words include more than one diphthong? Only the last three? Remember [e, i, u, o] are frequently diphthongized into [eɪ, ɪi, uu, ou]. Do not let the present use of the single symbols make you forget that the sounds thus represented are frequently diphthongs. In which of the three words incorporating the [e] sound does this sound appear *least* diphthongized? Why?

EXERCISE 62

Transcribe the following:

1. foul-mouthed _____

2. sounded _____

3. shouted _____

4. spouse _____

5. workout _____

6. gout _____

7. proud _____

8. confounding _____

9. resounding _____

10. accountancy _____

11. drowsily _____

12. whereabouts _____

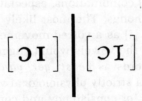

The diphthong [ɔɪ], as in the words *oil*, *toil*, and *spoil*, is produced by rapidly shifting the tongue from its low-back humped position forward and upward toward the [i] or [ɪ] position while emitting a vocalized air stream. Remember that this changing sound unit functions phonemically, so we react to it as *one* vocalic unit. The [ɔɪ] is a *fronting diphthong*.

DRILL

Practice writing the diphthong [ɔɪ] by creating ten words which include this sound:

_____

_____

_____

EXERCISE 63

Transcribe the following:

1. soil _____   10. oilstone _____

2. loiter _____   11. counterpoint _____

3. spoilt _____   12. royalty _____

4. boiled _____   13. Negroid _____

5. poise _____   14. boisterous _____

6. devoid _____   15. poinsettia _____

7. parboil _____   16. trapezoid _____

8. oiler _____   17. point-blank _____

9. viceroy _____   18. foisted _____

Certain phoneticians have considered other sound combinations as diphthongs. In particular, the [j] combinations, especially the [ju], have been considered by some to be diphthongs. The most likely basis for viewing [ju] as a diphthong is to consider the [j] as a voiced movement and hence a semivowel. However, placing [j] among the vowels would suggest that vowels (and hence diphthongs) initiate such words as *yeast, yet, yawn, yacht* and possibly *we, weigh, woo.* Although from a strictly physiological viewpoint the [j] movement is diphthongal in character, for consistency and convenience we will consider [j] as a glide consonant initiation of a vowel in this book.

Centering Diphthongs

Some other sound combinations, not yet discussed in this book, meet our criteria for consideration as diphthongs. These are the *centering diphthongs* [ɪɚ, ɛɚ, ɑɚ, ɔɚ, oɚ, ʊɚ]. (Figure 8 illustrates the tongue movements for these sounds.) The final element of each of these sound combinations is sometimes referred to as the *postvocalic r.* Some phoneticians argue that this sound should be transcribed after vowels as [ɪr, ɛr, ɑr, ɔr, or, ʊr]. This is the transcription used in the Kenyon and Knott dictionary. Both systems of notation have staunch adherents.

Let us first consider these combinations as *centering diphthongs.* No matter where the tongue is humped – either forward for the [ɪ] and [ɛ] sounds or toward the back for the [ɑ, ɔ, o, ʊ] sounds – it moves toward the middle for the final

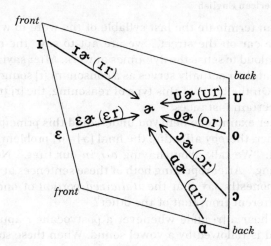

Fig. 8. Chart of the tongue movements for the centering diphthongs.

[ɚ] component. In our discussion of the [ɝ] and [ɚ] sounds, we noted that the tongue humped toward the center of the mouth. Hence the term *centering*, which suggests the voiced transition from either a front or back vowel to the central [ɚ]. Why not [ɪɝ, ɛɝ,...]? To find the answer, consider the beginning and the end of a diphthong separately for a moment. The emphasis, or stress, is always on the first component of a diphthong, rather than the second. Thus, the unstressed [ɚ] symbol is used instead of the stressed [ɝ],[2] and in words such as *car, ear, air, oar,* and *boor* we blend the given vowel with the concluding [ɚ] sound.

Research support for considering the postvocalic r as a vocalic element (and hence transcribing it as [ɚ]) can be derived from certain findings of Curtis and Hardy (1959). These investigators found that the sounds substituted for the postvocalic r were always vowels and were generally the same vowels as those substituted for [ɝ] and [ɚ]. Furthermore, a vowel (the schwa) is substituted for the postvocalic r by people with normal articulation who incorporate no r-coloring in their speech. In such speech, the word *poor* is pronounced [puə], *pair* is [pɛə], and *fierce* is [fɪəs]. If the r were properly performing the function of a consonant, it would be difficult to account for this substitution of a vowel. Such factors as regional usage and the way in which children misarticulate these sounds seem to offer strong support for considering postvocalic r sounds as vowels.

On the other hand, many phoneticians regard the postvocalic r as a consonant glide, transcribing it as [ɪr, ɛr, ɔr, bur]. Let us examine one justification for this transcription.

In the rhythmic flow of continuous speech our words tend to lose their individual identity and become blended together. Frequently the final sound of a word, when used in a sentence, serves to initiate the first syllable of the following

2. Similarly, in producing the diphthong [aɪ], the tongue rises only high enough to form the sound [ɪ], instead of ending on a stressed [i].

word rather than terminate the last syllable of the word to which it belongs. In the phrase "the car on the street," we are apt to say "the ca ron the street." Try saying this aloud to sense the dynamics at work. After saying it several times, you will note that the *r* actually serves as a consonant [r] sound initiating the [ɑn] vocal impulse. On the basis of this type of reasoning, the [r] transcription might be justified in certain instances.

Here is another example to help you understand this principle of *blending* one word into another, thereby affecting the final [ɚ] – [r] problem. Say the following sentence aloud: "We talk about having *air in* our tires." Now say: "Come to *Erin in* the spring." After repeating both of these sentences at a normal speaking rate, can you honestly say that the *italicized* portion of one sentence sounds significantly different from that of the other?

Many people hear a [r] glide whenever a postvocalic r appears in the middle of a phrase and is followed by a vowel sound. When these sound combinations appear at the end of a phrase or thought group or when *r* is followed by a consonant sound, as in [haɚt] and [kɔɚd], the [ɚ] transcription seems more valid. By defining [r] as a consonant glide, we would seem to be restricting it to a prevocalic function, thereby precluding its use in these words. It is to be noted, however, that the Kenyon and Knott phonetic dictionary gives the transcriptions [hɑrt] and [kɔrd].

A similar position – but one favoring the use of [r] – could be taken in favor of restricting the use of [ɚ] to a syllabic function. Yet we do not set up this added restriction for [ɪ] and [ʊ] with respect to the other diphthongs.

Your instructor will probably have some added opinions on this argument and may wish to influence you to use one transcription in preference to the other. In spite of the author's preference for the [ɚ] transcription, in this book we will follow the Kenyon and Knott transcriptions.

EXERCISE 64: TROUBLESOME WORDS

For each of the following words, alternative pronunciations are given. For each word, circle the pronunciation most commonly accepted as correct:

1. poignancy   a. [pɔɪgnənsɪ]   b. [pɔɪnənsɪ]

2. quietus   a. [kwaɪətəs]   b. [kwaɪitəs]

3. recognize   a. [rɛkəgnaɪz]   b. [rɛkənaɪz]

4. sinecure   a. [sɪnəsjʊr]   b. [sɪnɪkjʊr]

5. stipend   a. [stɪpənd]   b. [staɪpɛnd]

6. streptomycin   a. [strɛptomaɪosɪn] b. [strɛptomaɪsɪn]

EXERCISE 65

Since you have now learned all of the sound symbols necessary for phonemic transcription of the American English language, you are ready to complete the transcription of the names of the United States begun in Exercise 45:

1. Arizona _____
2. Arkansas _____
3. California _____
4. Colorado _____
5. Florida _____
6. Georgia _____
7. Hawaii _____
8. Idaho _____
9. Illinois _____
10. Iowa _____
11. Louisiana _____
12. Massachusetts _____
13. Michigan _____
14. Minnesota _____
15. Missouri _____
16. Montana _____
17. New Hampshire _____
18. New Jersey _____

19. New Mexico _____
20. New York _____
21. North Carolina _____
22. North Dakota _____
23. Ohio _____
24. Oklahoma _____
25. Oregon _____
26. Pennsylvania _____
27. Rhode Island _____
28. South Carolina _____
29. South Dakota _____
30. Utah _____
31. Vermont _____
32. Virginia _____
33. Washington _____
34. West Virginia _____
35. Wisconsin _____
36. Wyoming _____

EXERCISE 65: DISCUSSION

Transcribing this list must have raised some questions if you are at all responsive to the sounds we make when we talk. Did you hesitate on the vowel sound to be used in the word *New*? What is the correct vowel in the first syllable of *Florida* and *Oregon*? Which vowel did you use to begin the word *Arizona*? The various acceptable transcriptions for these states can be found in the phonetic dictionary.

EXERCISE 66: THE PASSAGE OF THE RAINBOW

Fill in the blanks:

It had been a particularly brilliant and spectacular storm, of comparatively long duration. Although storms of this type are seldom long remembered, this one was different. It had attracted and held the attention of many beholders. Now that the height of the frenzy was over, man's attention began to focus elsewhere. Like many such storms, however, this one had a wonderful aftermath – a resplendent rainbow. I personally can remember seeing [r____d, jɛ____, b____u, g____n, p____l, ____ndʒ, bl____k, br____n, hw____, ____re, p____k, g____d n sɪl____ kʌləᵘz]. There were some who swore they could identify shades of [lɛm____, laɪ____, ____lɪv, ɛmæ____d ṇ sæ____.] Others, however, disputed these aspects of the rainbow's passage. In any case, this many-hued spectacle certainly made a lasting impression. It still exerts its fascination in moments of contemplation. Strange, isn't it, how elusive that pot of gold still remains?

— With apologies to some colorful phoneticians

[t ʃæptɚ sʌməɪ]

[wɪð:ɪs tʃæptɚz dɪskʌʃən əv ðə dɪfθɔŋz aɪ, aʊ, ṇd ɔɪ, ju əv kənkludɪd jɚ stʌdɪ əv ɔl ðə fonimz juzd ɪn əmɛrəkən ɪŋglɪʃ. kɛrfəl kəmplɪʃən əv ðə mɛnɪ ɛksɚsaɪzɪz ʃud əv ɪmpruvd jɚ trænskrɪpʃən əbɪlətɪz. ətɛntɪv stʌdɪ ʃud əv əfɔrdɪd ju ṇ ʌndɚstændɪŋ əv ðə prabləmz ɪnvalvd ɪn trænskraɪbɪŋ postvokælɪk arz. ɪn ɔl prabəbɪlətɪ ju əv ɔlso ɪmpruvd jɚ prənʌnsieʃən əv səm trʌbḷsəm wɝdz.]

chapter 8

PHONETIC CROSSWORD PUZZLES AND WORD GAMES

Since the working of phonetic crossword puzzles seems to be effective in help-ing students think in terms of *sounds*, the following series of puzzles is in-cluded for both instruction and entertainment purposes. These crossword puzzles are intended to provide enjoyable practice, not to push back vocabulary frontiers. Accordingly, the words used are, for the most part, relatively common ones. Although the problems of puzzle construction have occasionally forced the use of an unusual word or two, esoteric words have been kept to a minimum.

The matter of accommodating regional dialects is not so great a problem as it might at first seem. An individual's vowel usage sometimes creates a conflict in the vowel intersection of such words as *sot* and *art* or *fob* and *yacht*. Occa-sionally the vowel in one word will force an alternative vowel pronunciation in the intersecting word. For example, in the intersection of the first vowels in *arrow* and *teller*, it is assumed that the [ɛ] in *teller* will force an [ɛ] – rather than an [æ] – initiation of *arrow*.

The major dialect problem will be experienced by people who do not use *r*-coloring. For this group, the problem will be most pronounced in such intersec-tions as *art* and *tree*, where the second word demands a consonant *r* in the space which might conceivably bear a [:] to show phonemically significant elongation of the [ɑ] in the intersecting word *art*. (Further discussion of [:] appears on page 145.)

Here are a few rules which should help you complete the following puzzles satisfactorily:

1. The blanks are to be filled in with phonetic symbols, not word spellings.
2. Diphthongs and the affricates [tʃ] and [dʒ] should take up one space only.
3. The sequence [ju] is not considered a diphthong, and hence should take up two spaces.
4. Postvocalic r's are to be transcribed with the [r] symbol, in accord with Kenyon and Knott.
5. The [l], [m], and [n] sounds may be syllabic consonants in one direction, yet *not* syllabic in the intersecting word containing the consonant in common.
6. The [ɪ] symbol may represent, in one direction, the vowel sound in *hit*, while serving, in the intersecting word, as the final -*y* sound in words like *party*.

Should you find yourself unable to complete a given puzzle or wish to check your work, there is at the end of this chapter an alphabetized list of all the words used in the puzzles (pages 130-134).

PUZZLE 1

əkrɔs

1. ə tʃembɚ fɚ bekɪŋ, hitɪŋ ɚ draɪɪŋ
4. tu wedʒɚ
7. ə rɪsɛptəkļ juzd fɚ prɪzɚvɪŋ ðɪ æʃɪz əv ðə dɛd æftɚ krɪmeʃən
8. ə nat, nab, protjubərəns, ɚ swɛlɪŋ
11. fɪr ɪnspaɪrɪŋ
12. glædnɪs, hæpɪnɪs, dɪlaɪt
13. ə wɛl non klaɪmɪŋ vaɪn
14. tə mek fɚm, stebļ, ɚ fæst
16. sɛkənd wɚd əv lætņ frez minɪŋ jɪrlɪ
18. wʌn bɪfɔr etθ
22. əbʌv
23. ə vɚtɪkļ səpɔrt
24. ðə grup əv simən hu mæn ə ʃip
25. hɪts wɪθ fɔrs
27. ə hom rʌn
29. ə prifɪks pɚtenɪŋ tə fɪʃ
32. ə wʊdwɪnd ɪnstrəmənt wɪð ə dʌbļ rid
33. ovɚhwɛlmɪŋ sɔro
35. ðə nʌmbɚ dɪnotɪŋ junətɪ
36. ə kənsɪdrəbļ ɪnlənd badɪ əv stændɪŋ wɔtɚ
37. ɪnspaɪɚd wɪθ ɔ
38. ə karpəntɚz tul fɚ bɔrɪŋ holz
39. ɛskɔrtɪd tu ə sit ɪn ə tʃɚtʃ ɚ θiətɚ

daʊn

2. ə bɔrdɚ, lɪmɪt, ɚ baʊndrɪ
3. tə dɪstɚb ɚ ɪrətet
4. slæŋ fɚ ə blo
5. ʌv ɚ pɚtenɪŋ tu ðɪ ɛr
6. hwʌt ə klɑk dʌz
8. nɛkst ɪn ɔrdɚ æftɚ ðɪ etθ
9. plʊrəl əv ovəm
10. nat braɪt
15. ə bætən ɔr stæf bɔrn baɪ ə savrɪn æz ņ ɛmbləm əv əθɔrətɪ

16. ðə stet əv səsaɪətɪ hwɛr ɜˑɹ ɪz no
    lɔ ɔr səprim pauɚ
17. tə kuk ɛgz ɪn sɪmərɪŋ wɔtɚ
19. tə tʃɛndʒ daɪrɛkʃən
20. tə dʒɔm baɪ ən əlaɪəns
21. nɜˑɹɪʃmənt tekən ɪn salɪd fɔrm
25. tʊ ɪnhel ənd ɛkshel ðə fjumz əv
    təbæko

26. æn əmɛrɪkən ɪndɪən wumən
27. æn openɪŋ ɪntʊ ɚ θru ɛnɪθɪŋ
28. tʊ bi əbidɪənt tu
30. ə kʌtθrot ɚ rʌfɪən
31. ɪntɜˑnl̩
33. tə klɛnz baɪ ðɪ æpləkeʃən əv
    ə lɪkwɪd
34. ə smɛl ɚ sɛnt

PUZZLE 2

əkrɔs

1. ə sɝkjələ strʌktʃɚ ɪn hwɪtʃ fadɚ gren, ɚ ʌðɚ fud ɪz stɔrd grin tə bɪ prɪzɝvd
5. ðə kraɪ əv ə waɪld bist
7. ən ɝb jildɪŋ ən ɔɪl juzd ɪn lɪkɝz
11. wʌn hu əfɛkts ɪkstrim madəstɪ ņ prəpraɪətɪ
12. ə dɪvaɪs fɚ fɝnɪʃɪŋ ən artəfɪʃəl: aɪt
13. ə kəmpɛtətɪv traɪl əv spid
14. ən arm əv ðə si
16. ðə floɪŋ bæk əv ðə taɪd tɔrd ðə si
18. apəzɪt əv bɔɪ
19. pæst əv ɪt
20. tu ɪntɛnd
21. wʌn əv ðə tu mʌskjələ ɔrgənz ðæt baʊnd ðə maʊθ ņ kʌvɚ ðə tiθ
23. dip, lɔŋdrən rɛspərɛʃən ɪksprɛsɪŋ sɔro, grif, fətig
24. swɪft
25. ə strʌktʃɚ ɪrɛktɪd tu əfɔrd pæsɪdʒ əkrɔs ə wɔtɚwe
27. ə krevɪŋ fɚ lɪkwɪdz
29. tɛrəfaɪŋ æntɪsəpeʃən
31. ə lardʒ dɪr wɪð pælmetɪd æntlɚz
32. ə frut huz blasəm ɪz ðə stet flaʊr əv arkənsɔ ņ mɪʃəgən

34. nɑt fæst
35. ɛnəmɪ
36. tə skɛtʃ, æz wɪθ pɛn ɚ pɛnsɪl
37. tu pəzɛs
38. ðə blit əv ə ʃip
40. ðə prɛzn̩t ɪndɪkətɪv plurəl əv ðə vɝb bi
43. nɑt fɑm ɚ dɛləkɪt
45. ɛnɪθɪŋ dɑunɪ ɚ fɛðɚɪ
47. ovɚ ənd ɪn kɑntækt wɪð
49. ən ɝb juzd ɪn pɪklɪŋ kjukʌmbɚz
50. wʌn əv ðə bonz hwɪtʃ fɔrm ðə wɔlz əv ðə θɔræks
51. æŋgɚ
52. tə dɪsɪnkʌmbɚ
54. tə sten
55. ðə waɪf əv ædəm
56. ə klaɪmɪŋ vaɪn
57. tə wɔk wɪrɪlɪ
60. ə flæt bɑtəmd fret bot
61. tu ɪnspɛkt
62. tə fɔl frəm ðə klaudz ɪn draps əv wɔtɚ
63. fimel nem

daun

1. tə wikən ə dʒɔɪnt ɚ mʌsl̩ baɪ sʌdən ɪksɛsɪv ɪgzɝʃən
2. ræθful
3. frid frəm nɔrml̩ bɑndz ɚ rɪstrent
4. wəz ɪndɛtɪd tu
6. ɛksklɑmeʃən ɪndəketɪŋ ə slaɪt pen
7. nɪknem fɚ ælbɚt
8. tu ɪrətet baɪ pɚsɪstənt skoldɪŋ ɚ ɝdʒɪŋ
9. tə plʌndʒ ɪntu ə fluɪd

10. tə junaɪt tu rops baɪ ɪntɚwivɪŋ ðə strændz
14. ɛnɪ fɔr futɪd ænəml̩
15. sʌbstænɖɚd fɚ æm nɑt
16. ə rɪvɚ ɪn dʒɝməni
17. ðə hɛr ɑn ə mænz tʃɪn
20. ə kʌvɚ fɚ ðə fes
22. tə pɛnətret ɚ pʌŋktʃɚ wɪθ ə pɔɪntɪd ɪnstrəmənt
24. liv əv æbsn̩s græntɪd tu ə soldʒɚ ɚ selɚ
26. ðə brænd nem əv ə dʒɛlətn̩
27. lɑrsn̩ɪ
28. ə drɑmə, holɪ ɚ mostlɪ sʌŋ, wɪθ ɔrkɛstrəl əkʌmpnɪmənt ənd əproprɪɪt kɑstjumz, sinrɪ, n̩d ækʃən
30. kəntrækʃən əv du nɑt
32. kəlokwɪəl fɚ ədvɝtɪzmənt
33. ə lɛdʒɪsletɪv ɪnæktmənt
38. tə pɔrtend
39. pɑrtʃt wɪθ hit
40. ə dʌl, grinɪʃ jɛlo kʌlɚ
41. tə pɑlɪʃ, bɝnɪʃ, ɚ braɪtn̩ baɪ frɪkʃən
42. pɔrʃənz

44. kræftɪ
45. nɑt baund baɪ rɪstrɪkʃənz
46. spænd
48. mɔr klos
51. ɛləfənt tʌsk
53. ə pɪdʒən
56. æn ætəm ɚ ə grup əv ætəmz bɛrɪŋ ən ɪlɛktrɪk tʃardʒ
58. tɛnθ lɛtɚ ɪn ðɪ ɪŋglɪʃ ælfəbɛt
59. ə nɛgətɪv vot ɚ votɚ
60. ðə sɛkənd lɛtɚ ɪn ðɪ ɪŋglɪʃ ælfəbɛt

PUZZLE 3

1	2		3			4	5	6					7	8
9		10				11	·					12		
	13		14	15		16				17	18			
	19					20				21				
22		23			24				25					26
27					28	29	30	31					32	
		33			34						35	36		
37	38			39		40				41		42	43	
44			45										46	
47		48	49								50	51		
52							53							

əkrɔs

1. m, ɑn, ɚ baɪ
3. rɪletɪŋ tu ən ɔrkɪstrə
7. bim əv laɪt
9. ə ʃɛl, hʌsk, ɚ pad
11. ə luk kənveɪŋ ə slaɪ, sɪnɪstɚ, ɔr ɪmadɪst səgdʒɛstʃən
12. tə pɚsu
13. rʌbd wɪθ sop
16. sʌmθɪŋ ðæt lidz tə ðə səluʃən əv ə mɪstrɪ
17. lɔŋ nɛro spesɪz fɚ bolɪŋ
19. ənklaʊdɪd
20. tə drɪŋk slolɪ ɪn smɔl əmaunts
21. hæd əfɛkʃən fɔr
23. drɔ fluɪd frʌm
25. ə krɪstʃən fɛstəvl̩ kəmɛməretɪŋ ðə rɛzərɛkʃən əv kraɪst
27. ə hardɪ, ænjuəl, sɪrɪəl græs kʌltəvetɪd æz ə fud gren
28. trʌstwɚði

32. nɑt ɪn
33. ðə taɪm ðæt ɛnɪθɪŋ hæz lɪvd ɚ ɪgzɪstɪd
34. ə tɛrətɔrɪ ovɚ hwɪtʃ dəmɪnjən ɪz ɛksɚsaɪzd
35. ə sɔft mæs əv mɔɪsn̩d flaʊr ɔr mil mɪkst fɚ kukɪŋ ɪntu ə brɛd
37. ə saʊr lɛmən laɪk frut
40. ə ples əv ɪtɚnl̩ pʌnɪʃmənt
42. ðə kraɪ əv ə kak
44. ði ɪnhɛrətɪd, ɪnstɪŋktɪv ɪmpʌls əv ði ɪndəvɪdʒuəl
45. plest ɪn ɪlɛktrɪkl̩ kənɛkʃən wɪð: ɚθ
46. twɛlfθ lɛtɚ ɪn ði ɪŋglɪʃ ælfəbɛt
47. ə baɪvælv maləsk
50. bɪniθ
52. pɚtenɪŋ tu ə smɛd
53. ɪnakjələbl̩, ɪmjunaɪzɪŋ edʒənts

daʊn

1. ðə paʊdərɪ rɛsədju əv ə sʌbstəns ðæt hæz bɪn bɜˑnt
2. lɔŋ prətrudɪŋ ɛləfənt:uθ
4. lardʒ dɪrz wɪθ pælmɛtɪd æntlɚz
5. fulɪʃ
6. ə kʌmpənɪ əv trævl̩ɪŋ æktɚz
7. muvd ʌpwɚd
8. ə sɪŋgl̩ spɑt pleɪŋ kard
10. nɑt wɔrm
12. wʌn hu tʃɪrz
14. ðə nobɪlətɪ
15. ə flæt bɑtəmd rɪsɛptəkl̩ wɪθ ə lo rɪm fɚ kɛrɪŋ artɪkl̩z
17. ə tul fɚ tʃɑpɪŋ
18. vɜˑst ɪn lɛtɚz
22. mɜˑθfəl præŋks
24. ə fɔrwɚd ən daʊnwɚd moʃən əv ðə hɛd

25. ə fɛməs ɪŋglɪʃ kɑlɪdʒ
26. ðoz hu strol
29. sʌbstændɚd fɔr ɪn no we
30. væst
31. trævl̩d baɪ bot
33. tə pɔɪnt ə wɛpən æt ən ɑbdʒɪkt
36. ə hard wʊd ekɔrn bɛrɪŋ tri
38. ɪn ən aɪdl̩ mænɚ
39. ðə riprədʌktɪv badɪ prədust baɪ hɛnz
41. tu faɪnd ðə sʌm əv
43. tə mek rɛd
48. wʌn ɚ ɛnɪ
49. əbriviɛʃən fɚ mamə
50. ðɪ ɑbdʒɛktɪv kes plurəl əv ðə pɚsn̩l̩ pronaʊn əv ðə fɜˑst pɚsn̩
51. ðə dʒɔɪnt əv ðə hjumən lɛg mɪdwe bɪtwin ðə hɪp dʒɔɪnt ən ðɪ æŋkl̩

PUZZLE 4

(crossword grid with numbered cells 1–56)

əkrɔs

2. nɛgətɪv ɪmɪdʒ kapɪz
9. nɪr ðə bɪgɪnɪŋ əv ə pɪrɪəd əv taɪm
12. ðɪ ʌpɚ part əv ðə lɛg frəm ðə hɪp tə ðə ni
13. nɔɪz əv ə kaʊ
14. sɛkənd sʌn əv ædəm
16. tu rɔr æz ə bʊl
18. ðə swɛl əv ðə si ðæt breks əpan ðe ʃɔr
20. ə fɪlm fɔrmd əpan stægnənt ɚ faʊl wɔtɚ
21. ɛkspɚtnəs
23. wənz faðɚz ɚ mʌðɚz brʌðɚ
25. nat frɛʃ
26. ɪn ɪŋglənd, skatlənd, ənd aɪɚlənd, mɛn əv nobɪləti ræŋkɪŋ nɛkst bɪlo marki ən:ɛkst əbʌv vaɪkaunt
28. ðɪ æksʃən ɚ prasɛs əv lɔntʃɪŋ ə vɛsl̩
30. dʒɛst
32. ðə pɪrɪəd bətwin tʃaɪldhʊd n̩ ədʌlt edʒ
34. ən ɝθɪ mətɪrɪəl juzd ɪn mekɪŋ patɚi
37. tu θro ɪntu dɪsɔrdɚ ɔr kənfjuʒən
40. ən ɪnklozd ples hwɛr swaɪn ɚ kɛpt
42. ə lɛŋkθ əv strɔŋ n̩ staʊt laɪn ɚ kɔrdɪdʒ juʒuəli med əv twɪstɪd strændz əv hɛmp, flæks, ɚ ʌðɚ faɪbrəs mətɪrɪəl
43. ə wʊdn̩, dʌbl̩ rid mjuzɪkl̩ ɪnstrəmənt
44. nɪknem əv arθɚ
45. ʌnkwaləfaɪd, ʌnkəndɪʃənl̩
48. ðə kardn̩əl nʌmbɚ kəmpozd əv tɛn ən sɪks
51. ə dɔtɚ əv wʌnz brʌðɚ ɚ sɪstɚ
53. nat fɔls

54. prɪkt ən mɑrkt wɪθ ɪndɛləbḷ pɪgmənts
55. ə stet, savrɪn, ɚ tʃif ligd wɪθ ənʌðɚ baɪ triti ɚ kamən ækʃən
56. luzɪŋ taɪm ɪn aɪdḷnəs

daʊn

1. tu rɪstren
3. ə saləm əpil tə gɑd ɪn wɪtnɪs ðæt ə stetmənt ɪz tru
4. ə krəvæt
5. ðæt hwɪtʃ ɪnsaɪts ɔr ɚdʒɪz
6. fɚst pɚsṇ sɪŋgjələ prɛznt ɪndɪkətɪv əv ðə vɚb tə bi
7. ɔlso
8. ə ʃed tri wɪθ ə brɔd, sprɛdɪŋ, ɚ ovɚ artʃɪŋ tap
10. kəntrækʃən əv lɛt ʌs̩
11. sɪk
14. tə sʌfɚ dʌl kəntɪnjud pen
15. ə klʌstɚ
17. ɪndɪən traɪb
18. tə dɪspɛrɪdʒ ɚ dɪpriʃɪet
19. fam laɪt partɪkḷz ɚ faɪbɚz
20. həbɪtʃuəl lezɪnɪs

22. ə lus aʊtɚ garmənt
24. ɪndɪkeʃənz ðæt lid tə ðə səluʃən əv ə mɪstrɪ
27. spɛndz taɪm ɪn aɪdlnɪs
29. skrept ɔr:ʌbd tu əle ɪrəteʃən
31. ə kəndʌktɚz kar an ə fret:ren
32. ə part əv ən ægrɪgɪt
33. ə sʌdṇ flæʃ əv laɪt kɔzd baɪ ðə dɪstʃardʒ əv ɪlɛktrɪsəti bɪtwin tu ɪlɛktrəfaɪd ridʒənz əv klaud ɚ bɪtwin ə klaud ṇ ðɪ ɚθ
35. ə raundɪd prodʒɛkʃən əv ən orgən ɚ part
36. mʌŋkɪz
38. smɔl ɪnsɛkt ɚ flaɪ
39. ɪmplɔɪmənt
40. ə həbɪtʃuəl drʌŋkɚd
41. ə wudɪ plænt hævɪŋ ə sɪŋgḷ trʌŋk kamənlɪ ɪksidɪŋ. tɛn fit ɪn haɪt
46. ovɚ əgɛn
47. tə prɪsid ən dərɛkt ɪn muvmənt
49. tə wip
50. ɪnstətjutɪd ligḷ prɛsidɪŋz
52. tə lubrɪket

PUZZLE 5

əkrɔs

1. ə smɔl nu ɪŋglənd stet
6. nat ən
7. ə rɪspɛktfəl taɪtl̩ juzd ɪn ədrɛsɪŋ ə mæn wɪθaut juzɪŋ hɪz nem
9. tə klat ɚ kəndʒil
10. mɔr ðæn wʌn ænəml̩ θaɪməs ɚ pæŋkriəs juzd fɚ fud
16. kampənseʃən fɚ prəfɛʃənl̩ sɚvɪs
18. ðə mɪsl̩ wɛpən juzd wɪθ ə bo
19. tə præktɪs ɛtʃɪŋ
20. ðə hol nʌmbɚ ɚ sʌm əv
21. ə smɔl wɪŋləs ɪnsɛkt hwɪtʃ sʌks ðə blʌd əv wɔrm blʌdɪd ænəmlz
22. ə pɚsn̩ əv ðə hibru res
23. wʌn hu gɪvz ɚ donets
24. ə soʃəl grup kəmpraɪzɪŋ ə sɪriz əv fæmlɪz, klænz, ɚ dʒɛnəreʃənz, təgɛðɚ wɪθ slevz, ədaptɪd strendʒɚz, ɛt sɛtərə
26. stet əv biɪŋ səprim
30. tə səspɛnd ə sɛʃən fɚ rɪzʌmpʃən æt ənʌðɚ taɪm ɚ ples
31. fimel nem
32. ðə stet an ðə mɛksɪkən frʌntɪr laɪɪŋ bɪtwin ærəzonə n̩ tɛksɪs

daun

1. ə mitɪŋ əv mɛmbɚz əv ə pəlɪtɪkl̩ partɪ tə dɪsaɪd an paləsɪz ɚ kændədets
2. tu wɚdz dɛzɪgnetɪŋ ən ɛnəmɪ
3. tu əprez krɪtɪklɪ
4. rɛptl̩z hævɪŋ ə bonɪ ʃɛl hwɪtʃ ɪnklozɪz ðə trʌŋk ænd ɪntu hwɪtʃ

ɔl ðə mɛmbɚz me bɪ drɔn fɚ
prətɛkʃən

5. ə stet hævɪŋ ə nɔrθ ŋ̩ sauθ lɛŋkθ
əv sɛvn̩ hʌndrɪd ŋ̩ fɪftɪ maɪlz

8. ðə stet most ɪntəmɪtlɪ əsoʃɪetɪd
ɪn əmɛrəkən maɪndz wɪð:ɪ ɚlɪ
hɪstrɪ əv ðə rɪpʌblɪk

11. tə rol wʌnsɛlf əbaut æz ɪn maɪɚ

12. wʌn hu tɛlz

13. ðə fɔrhɛd

14. tə kuk ɪn ən ʌvən

15. kɑntrədɪkt

17. ə fɪʃ əv ɪlɔŋgetɪd snek laɪk fɔrm

19. brɪŋk ɚ vɚdʒ

23. tu dɪtɛkt

25. tred nem əv pædz juzd fɚ klinɪŋ,
skaurɪŋ, ŋ̩ pɑlɪʃɪŋ

27. ovɚ əgɛn

28. ə lɑrdʒ dɪr wɪθ pælmetɪd æntlɚz

29. ə bæg

PUZZLE 6

əkrɔs

3. ðə læŋgwɪdʒ əv dɛnmɑrk
9. ə lɑrdʒ bɝd əroniəslɪ sɛd tə bɛrɪ ɪts hɛd ɪn ðə sænd hwɛn ɪn dɛndʒɝ
11. ə klɝdʒɪmən əfɪʃəlɪ ətætʃt tu ðɪ ɑrmɪ ɚ nevɪ
13. ðə suprim diətɪ əv ðɪ enʃənt griks
14. ɪn besbɔl, ðə pleɚz hu ɚ nɑt hævɪŋ ðɛr ɪnɪŋz
15. tə hɪndɚ frʌm nɔrml̩ groθ
20. æn əmɛrɪkən ɪndiən wumən
22. ə fɑloɚ əv ðɪ jogə fɪlɑsəfɪ
24. mɪdwɛstɚn sɪtɪ wɝld femd fɚ ɪts bɪr
25. ə fɔlshud
27. wʌn hu ɪtʃɪz
28. tu əprez

29. tu ɪmətet æbsɝdlɪ ɔr slevɪʃlɪ
30. ʌnɛsəsɛrɪ æktɪvətɪ
32. nɪknem fɚ ɪzikɪəl
34. mɛrɪmənt
35. nɪknem fɚ zækərɑɪə
37. trævl̩ θru ðɪ ɛr
39. tu ɪmɪt ə kɝənt əv ɛr
41. wʌn əv ə trɑɪb əv ɪndiənz mostlɪ lɪvɪŋ ɑn ə rɛzɚveʃən ɪn ærəzonə, nu mɛksəko, ænd jutɔ
42. ə stet wɪθ liniənt dɪvɔrs lɔz

daʊn

1. æt hom ɪn ɛnɪ kʌntrɪ
2. ə sɪriəl græs feməs ɪn ðə fɔrm əv mil
3. plʌndʒɪz ɪntə lɪkwɪd

4. etθ lɛtɚ əv ælfəbɛt
5. tə hæv ən ʌnizɪ sɛnse ʃən ɪn ðə skɪn
6. kəlokwɪəl kəntrækʃən əv ʃæl nɑt
7. tə tɪl ðɪ ɝθ
8. ə wɝk kəntenɪŋ ɪnfɚmeʃən ɑn ɑl sʌbdʒɪkts ɔr ɪgzɔstɪv əv wʌn sʌbdʒɪkt
10. tə prasɪkjut dʒudɪʃəlɪ
12. ðə njutɚ pronaun əv ðə θɝd pɝsn sɪŋgjələ
16. pɪpl̩ ɚ bots ðæt fɪʃ ɚ drɛdʒ baɪ trɔlɪŋ
17. sɪtɪ feməs fɚ skaɪ skrepɚz
18. ðə kʌlməneʃən

19. ə vəraɪətɪ əv kwɔrts juzd ɪn mekɪŋ marblz̩
21. sɔrsərɪs
23. kəlokwɪəl ɪkspreʃən sɪgnəfaɪɪŋ əpruvl̩
26. kəntrækʃən əv aɪ wʊd
29. ə kaɪnd əv bɪr
31. tu ɪgzjud mɔɪstʃɚ
33. ə foldɪŋ frem fɚ səportɪŋ ə pɪktʃɚ
34. ə fɛlo
36. tɪtʃɚ ɪn saɪæm med feməs baɪ bʊk ən mjuzɪkl̩
38. ardṇt əfɛkʃən
39. ə bɛnt ɚ kɝvd wɛpən
40. tə pəzɛs

PUZZLE 7

1	▓	2	3	4	▓	5	6	7	▓ 8
9	10				▓	11			12
13			▓		▓		14		
15			▓	16		17			
18		▓	19		20	▓	21		
22	▓	23			▓	24	▓	25	
▓	26			▓	▓		▓	27	
▓	28			▓	▓	29	▓	30	▓
31		▓	32	▓	33		34		35
36		▓	37	▓	38	39			
▓	40			▓	41		▓		

əkrɔs

2. tə kəmpit ɪn spid
5. trænsgrɛʃən əv ðə lɔ əv gad
9. kʌt ɔf
11. brɪtɪʃ nem fɚ məlæsɪz
13. əbriviɛʃən əv tɛknɪkl̩
14. karnəvl̩ kɔld mardɪ _____
15. ɪrətetɪd
17. saʊnd əv ə frɔg
18. ən ɔrgən fɚ rɛspərɛʃən̩ ʌndɚ wɔtɚ
19. ðə ʃɔr əv ðə si
21. slæŋ fɚ ɔlraɪt
22. ovɚ ænd ɪn kantækt wɪθ
23. dɪsəpɪr
25. hɛlp
26. smɔl fluts wɪθ tonz ən aktɪv haɪɚ ðæn ðoz əv ði ɔrdnɛrɪ flut
28. ðə tɪʃju hwɪtʃ səraʊndz ðə rut əv ə tuθ
29. ðæt hwɪtʃ ɪz dʌn
31. dɪsebl̩d ɪn ðə lɛg ɚ fut

34. ðə kraɪ əv ə dʌŋkɪ
36. wʌn tʃozn̩ tə rul an ðə plez əv ə gem
38. tə hɪt wɪθ sʌm fɔrs
40. pæst:ɛns əv sle
41. bɪldɚ əv ən ark

daʊn

1. ə palɪgan hævɪŋ et saɪdz
2. tə drɔ bæk ɚ fɔl bæk
3. ə lardʒ mʌŋkɪ
4. tə bɔɪl slolɪ
5. sɚkjələ moʃən wɪθ ə spun ɪn fluɪd
6. ði ɔrgən əv hɪrɪŋ
7. ə pɚsn̩ əv ðə blæk res
8. əbstrʌkʃənz tə nevl̩ pæsɪdʒ
10. rʌʃən rɛvəluʃ ənɪst
12. ə lɔn gem pled wɪθ bɔlz, mæ**l**ɪts, waɪr artʃɪz, n̩ steks
16. fevrɪt sɚkəs n̩ bɔlgem snæk

19. ɑpəzɪt əv frʌnt
20. ə sɛnseʃən əv kold ətɛndɪd wɪθ
    ʃɪvərɪŋ
23. ɛnɚdʒɛtɪk ɚ æktɪv pauɚ
24. dɪspled
26. dɪvaɪsɪz ðæt rez fluɪdz baɪ sʌkʃən
    ɚ prɛʃɚ ɔr boθ
27. ən æfrɪkən æslaɪk mæml̩ wɪθ
    dɑrk straɪps ɑn ə hwaɪt ɚ bʌf
    graund

28. ən əmjuzmənt ɚ dəvɝʒən
30. nɑt wɛt
31. fɛvrəbl̩ fɔrtʃən
32. frəm wʌn ɛnd tu ðɪ ʌðɚ
33. dʒɝmən mænjəfæktʃərɪŋ sɪtɪ
35. sʌfɚz kəntɪnjud pen
37. ə tʃɝtʃ ɚ θiətɚ pæsɪdʒwe baɪ
    hwɪtʃ ðə pjuz ɚ sits me bɪ ritʃt
39. wʌn əv ðə tɚmənl̩ mɛmbɚz ɔr
    dɪdʒɪts əv ðə fut

PUZZLE 8

		1	2			3	4			5	6	
7					8				9		10	
				11			12					
13	14	15							16	17		
18			19					20				
	21			22			23					
24			25		26	27				28	29	
30				31					32			
33			34					35		36		
		37						38	39			
40							41					

əkrɔs

1. bɛnt ɚ tɝnd bækwɚd
7. tə flɪŋ wʌnsɛlf əbaut æz ɪn slip
8. ɪlɛvənθ lɛtɚ ɪn ðɪ ɪŋglɪʃ ælfəbɛt
9. ən ɪlɛktrɪklɪ tʃɑrdʒd ætəm ɚ grup əv ætəmz
11. pæθədʒɛnɪk bæktɪrɪə
13. laɪklɪ
16. ə jutɛnsl̩ fɚ strenɪŋ
18. ə pramɪs
20. hwət skɪn dʌz hwɛn ɪkspozd tə ðə sʌn
21. tə ritʃ ə ples
23. tu ʃek wɪθ kold ɚ fɪr
24. ɪn, an, baɪ, ɚ nɪr tu
25. ə tred mark fɚ sɝtn̩ pətrolɪəm pradəkts
28. twɛntɪ sɛkənd lɛtɚ əv ðɪ ælfəbɛt
30. ə gɪtɑr laɪk mjuzɪkl̩ ɪnstrəmənt
31. tə θrʌst ə pɔɪntəd ɪmpləmənt

32. ə hʌzbənd ɚ waɪf
33. bɪŋ wɪðɪn
34. ə bɪldɪŋ fɚ ðɪ əkamədeʃən əv pæsn̩dʒɚz an relwe laɪnz
36. twɛntɪnθ lɛtɚ ɪn ðɪ ɪŋglɪʃ ælfəbɛt
37. tə prɪzɛnt tə saɪt
38. ɪn kes ðæt
40. ə tɛnənt farmɚ hu rɪsivz æz wedʒɪz ə ʃɛr əv ðə krap
41. goz wɪð ə stɛdɪ, dʒagɪŋ pes

daun

1. nat kukt
2. naɪntɪnθ lɛtɚ əv ðɪ ɪŋglɪʃ ælfəbɛt
3. hæpən
4. rɪnaun
5. grik lɛtɚ ɪndəketəd baɪ ɛks
6. ə rɪspɛktful taɪtl̩ æz prənaunst ɪn parts əv ðə sauθ

7. tʊ ɪnsnɛr
10. plʊrəl əv naɪf
11. wʌn əv ðə tu strʌktʃɚz fɔrmɪŋ ðə fremwɚk əv ðə maʊθ
12. ə mənædʒərɪ
14. ə sʌbdəvɪʒən əv ə mɪlətɛrɪ tæktɪkl̩ junɪt
15. pʊl əpart
16. ə hilɪŋ ɔɪntmənt
17. tə stɪmjələt θru nɝvz
19. swɪŋ mjuzɪk
20. hwət kænz ar med əv

22. ɪmɛns
23. ə kʌntrɪ əv saʊθ ərebɪə, febl̩d fɚ ɪts wɛlθ, huz kwin vɪzɪtɪd saləmən
24. ə lɔŋ nɛro spes fɚ bolɪŋ
26. tə rɪmen
27. ə strok wɪθ ə hwɪp
29. tu lɛtɚz əv ðɪ ælfəbɛt
34. ə klɛnzɪŋ edʒənt
35. klos
37. ðə taɪtl̩ əv ðə rulɚ ɪn ɪran
39. fɔrθ ton əv ðə daɪətanɪk skel

PUZZLE 9

	1	2			3	4			5	6			7
8				9				10				11	
		12				13				14			
	15				16				17				
18				19				20					21
22			23				24				25		
		26				27				28			
	29				30				31				
32				33				34					35
36			37				38				39		
		40				41				42			
	43				44				45				
46				47				48					

əkrɔs

1. nat lus
3. smɔl sɪŋɪŋ bɝd
5. tə bi ən faɪr
8. brɪtɪʃ ɚ aɪrɪʃ nobḷmən ræŋkɪŋ nɛkst bəlo ə marki an:ɛkst əbʌv ə vaɪkaunt
9. sist lɪvɪŋ
10. ə sɔŋ sʌŋ fɚ ə dɪpartɪd sol
11. twɛntɪ fɪfθ lɛtɚ əv ðɪ ɪŋglɪʃ ælfəbɛt
12. ə gud frɛnd ɚ kəmpænjən
13. ə sid vɛsḷ əv ə plænt
14. ə flɛksəbḷ kʌvrɪŋ fɚ ðə hɛd n̩ bæk əv ðə nɛk
15. əbdʒɛktɪv kes əv hi
16. ðə haɪnd part əv ðə hjumən fut
17. ə ræʃən fɚ ðə nidɪ
18. pæst:ɛns əv rʌn
19. obis
20. tu opən ðə mauθ waɪd əspɛʃəlɪ ɪnvaləntɛrəlɪ θru drauzɪnɛs, dʌlnɪs, ɚ fətig
22. hwaɪl
23. ə ʃɛltɚd kɔrnɚ ɚ ples
24. ə ʃɔrt wɔtʃ rɪbən ɚ tʃen
25. ðə fɪfθ mʌnθ əv ðə jɪr
26. tə brɪŋ tə ðə bɔɪlɪŋ pɔɪnt
27. ən ɪntəragətɪv rɪfɝɪŋ tə ðə netʃɚ ɔr aɪdɛntətɪ əv ən abdʒɪkt ɚ mætɚ ɪn kwɛstʃən

28. ə taɪp əv sɪŋkəpetɪd əmɛrɪkən mjuzɪk
29. ðɪ ɔrgən əv smɛl
30. mɛtrɪkl̩ raɪtɪŋ
31. ækt əv kʌmɪŋ ɪntə laɪf
32. tu əfɪks ə sɪgnətʃɚ
33. slæŋ fɔr tiz
34. ə smɔl, ʃɔrt, ʃarpːɔɪntɪd nel juʒuəlɪ hævɪŋ ə brɔd flæt hɛd
36. sɪksθ lɛtɚ ɪn ðɪ ɪŋglɪʃ ælfəbɛt
37. pæstːɛns əv mit
38. laɪəbɪlətɪ
39. saləm pramɪs
40. ə prɔŋd ɪnstrəmənt fɚ stɚɪŋ ənd sprɛdɪŋ ɚθ
41. tə dəmɪnɪʃ
42. ə laɪt blʌnt sɔrd fɚ fɛnsɪŋ
43. ə dɪmanstrətɪv pɔɪntɪŋ aᵘt sʌmθɪŋ prɛzn̩t ɪn taɪm, ples, ɚ θɔt
44. tu akjəpaɪ ə sit
45. hɛns
46. frut hævɪŋ ə fʌzɪ skɪn
47. æn ɪnflɛktɪd fɔrm əv tɛn ædɪd tə ðə numrəlz frəm θri tə naɪn tə fɔrm ðoz frəm θɚtin tə naɪntin
48. ðæt hwɪtʃ ɪz ped fɚ wɚk

daʊn

1. tə kɔz tə rɪvalv
2. kəntrækʃən əv aɪ wɪl
3. mek tə kɔrəspand ɪn saʊnd
4. ʃɔrt fɚ ɛdwɚd
5. ə wɪŋd, fɛðɚd, ɛg leɪŋ, vɚtəbret ænəml̩
6. tə fɔrs anwɚd
7. ʌtɚd ə fɔlshud
9. mjut
10. ə tɔɪ bebɪ fɚ ə tʃaɪld

11. ðə kot əv ʃip
12. ðə loɚ ɪkstrɛmətɪ əv ðə fes bɪlo ðə maʊθ
13. tɚf kʌt fɚ jus əz fjuəl
14. ə faɪn hwɛtston fɚ ʃarpənɪŋ ɛdʒd tulz
15. θɚd pɚsn̩ sɪŋgjəlɚ prɛzn̩t əv hæv
16. tə kʌt ɪrɛgjələⁱlɪ
17. tə pent ɪn ə kɔrs ɚ ʌnskɪlful mænɚ
18. ə rodn̩t
19. fɪld
20. ə smɔl vɛsl̩ juzd fɚ plɛʒɚ
21. tə fɪks ðɪ aɪz ɪn ə stɛdɪ n̩ ɪntɛnt luk
23. laʊd kənfjuzd ɚ sɛnsləs ʃaʊtɪŋ
24. tə frɪdʒɪt
25. əbriⁱɛʃən əv mæθəmætɪks
26. wʌn əv ðə hard pisɪz ɚ parts əv ðə skɛlətn̩ əv most vɚtəbrets
27. rɪvalvz kwɪklɪ wɪθ ə bʌzɪŋ ɚ hwɪzɪŋ saʊnd
28. ə ʃarp sʌdn̩lɪ ərɛstɪd pʊl
29. ə tebl̩ tul fɚ kʌtɪŋ
30. ə lardʒ vɛsl̩, sɪstɚn, tʌb, ɚ bɛrəl
31. ə klʌb juzd ɪn besbɔl
32. dɪspoz əv baɪ sel
33. ðə brokən rɪmenz əv ɛnɪθɪŋ rɛkt
34. nʌmbɚ æftɚ naɪn
35. əfɛnsɪv tə ðə sɛnsɪz
37. ə stæf bɔrn baɪ ə dɪgnətɛrɪ æz ən ɛnsɪn əv hɪz əθɔrətɪ
38. ðə frut əv ə pam
39. tu ʌtɚ
40. wɛlθɪ
41. tə gen ɪn kampətɪʃən ɚ kantɛst
42. ə sɔft ʃugərɪ kændɪ
43. ðɪ əbdʒɛktɪv kes əv ðaʊ
44. tə pɚsiv baɪ ðɪ aɪ
45. ðə plʊrəl əv hi, ʃi, ɚ ɪt

PUZZLE 10

əkrɔs

1. ə dɪtel
4. ðə kʌlmənefən
8. fɔrt fɚ koapərətɪv
9. pɚtenɪŋ tə ðə mun
11. ə dʒɝni
13. ə patbɛlɪ
15. ə dɪstɪŋktɪv ætməsfɪr səraundɪŋ ə pɚsn̩
16. stet əv rɛst
18. ə mɪstfɪvəs tfaɪld
19. læst lɛtɚ əv ælfəbɛt
21. tə brek ɚ kræk ɔf ə pɔrfən əv
22. kʌmfɚt
23. straɪv fɚ səpɪrɪɔrətɪ
25. nɪknem əv rɪsn̩t junaɪtɪd stets prɛzədənt
26. tə kɪl
28. ɔstrɪən batn̩ɪst feməs fɚ ɪz prɪnsəpl̩ əv hərɛdətɪ
31. bəlɔŋɪŋ tu ɪt
32. ðə fut əv ən ænəml̩
34. laɪk do
35. tə mɛrɪt ɚ dɪzɝv

36. artɪkl̩z əv fud med wɪð ə krʌst əv fɔrtn̩d do
37. rɛprɪzɛntefənz prədust baɪ pentɪŋ

daʊn

1. vɛrɪ smɔl kwantətɪz
2. ə selɚ
3. bɪkʌm vɪzəbl̩
5. farp nelz an ðə fɪŋgɚz ɚ toz əv ən ænəml̩
6. ðə sætl̩aɪt fɛdɪŋ most laɪt an ɝθ ət naɪt
7. mɔr ðæn wʌn ɪntf
10. ə sɛmɪfluɪd sop (tu wɝdz)
12. tə plʌndʒ fɔrwɚd n̩ daʊnwɚd laɪk ə fɪp
13. ðə hɛd əv ðə romən kæθlɪk tfɝtf
14. konɪfərəs ɛvɚgrin triz
17. ə pɚkʌsɪv strɪŋd mjuzɪkl̩ ɪnstrəmənt
20. ðɪ ivnɪŋ bɪfɔr ə fist
22. tə mek ə lɪvɪŋ ɪn skæntɪ fæfən

24. kəntrækʃən əv aɪ æm
25. ə smɔl aɪlənd
27. mɪmɪks
29. ə hwɝ·lpul

30. tə plʌndʒ ɚ ɪmɝ·s fɔr ə taɪm
31. ðə twɛlfθ pɑrt əv ə fut
33. ɪz baund baɪ mɔrəl ɑbləgeʃən
35. tu ənɔɪ

PUZZLE 11

əkrɔs

1. sɪmələ˞ tu ə tʃáɪm
6. ə flaʊərɪŋ plænt
9. tə kənvɜ˞t tə wʌnz sɜ˞vɪs
10. ɛksɛntrɪk
12. ʃrɪŋkɪŋ madəstlɪ frəm fəmɪlɪɛrətɪ
13. tʊ ɪgzjud mɔɪstʃɚ
14. ə bar juzd baɪ dʒɪmnæsts ņ æk-rəbæts
16. pipļ huz rɪlɪdʒən ɪz dʒudəɪzəm
17. ə pis əv nidḷwɚk wɪð ɪmbrɔɪdɚd lɛtɚz ɚ vɜ˞sɪz
19. tə rɪfjuz tʊ əlaʊ
20. ðə gren əv ə sɪrɪəl græs
21. lardʒ rɪsɛptəkļz fɔr holdɪŋ fluɪdz
22. pæst partəsɪpḷ əv ʃo
24. kloðɪŋ wɔrn tə protɛkt wənz pɜ˞sən ɪn bætḷ
25. ə kwɪvərɪŋ ɚ vaɪbrətɔrɪ moʃən
27. ðə kraɪz əv ə dʌŋkɪ
28. ə kraʊnlaɪk hɛd ɔrnəmənt
30. tʃuz ņ swɑloz
31. ðə dɪrɛkʃən əv sʌnraɪz
32. ðə taɪtḷ baɪ hwɪtʃ ə pɜ˞sən ɚ θɪŋ ɪz non

daʊn

1. ə dɪvaɪs fɚ tʃɑrdʒɪŋ stɔrɪdʒ bætrɪz
2. ðə namθ lɛtɚ əv ðɪ ɪŋglɪʃ ælfəbɛt
3. tə mɛdətet
4. tə sʌfɚ lɔs
5. ɔrgənz əv vɪʒən
7. wʌn hu skiz
8. θɪŋz tə ple wɪð
10. ə səspɛnʃən əv hɑstɪlətɪz baɪ əgrimənt
11. tə dəvɜ˞səfaɪ wɪθ spɑts
14. dutɪ ɔr tʃɔr
15. ðæt part əv ə plaʊ hwɪtʃ kʌts ðə fɜ˞o
17. wʌn hu sɪŋz
18. nʌmbɚ æftɚ sɛvən
19. bɛrɪɚz tə prɪvɛnt ðə flo əv wɔtɚ
20. wʌn hu onz
21. tə kɑpɪ an ə supɚpozd ʃɪt
23. ə fɔrbodɪŋ
24. næk ɚ skɪl ɪn pɚfɔrmənts
26. tə dɪke
27. tʊ ɪgzɪst
28. æn ærəmætɪk bɛvrɪdʒ
29. θɜ˞tinθ lɛtɚ ɪn ðɪ ɪŋglɪʃ ælfəbɛt

Word Game 1

Playing phonetic word games can be both exciting and exasperating. Long automobile trips are good for such activities, but a station wagon traveling sixty-five miles an hour with the windows open has rather poor acoustics. To compensate for such acoustic hazards, you may wish to use identification tags for certain sounds. The "two-bar [ɪ]," the "round-and-round [æ]," the "tailless [ʊ],"and the doctor's sound" ([ɑ]) have all proven helpful. The traditionally accepted designations of "epsilon" and "schwa" and their hooked relatives [ɝ] and [ɚ] are also helpful to players of phonetic games.

A favorite phonetic game is word building. The goal is for consecutive players to add a sound to those preceding, without completing a legitimate word. After the players determine a sequence for taking turns, the first player produces one of the phonemes used in the English language. The second player adds a sound to the first but attempts to do so without completing a two-phoneme word. In like manner, each successive player continues to add a sound to the preceding sound-sequence, trying not to terminate a legitimate word in the process. Players may not select sounds at random; they must have in mind a word which their additional sound would help create. If the player currently taking his turn thinks the previous player's addition does not further a legitimate word, he may challenge the preceding player. A challenged player who is unable to produce a word receives a demerit. A demerit is also received by any player who completes a word. Any previously agreed upon number of demerits puts a player out of the game.

The demerit score can be kept by numbers, or the numbers can be translated to a word. For example, a player who has completed only one word might be a [f]; upon completing a second word, or failing to satisfy a challenge, he becomes a [fo]; the third word or unsatisfied challenge makes him a [fon]; the fourth makes him a [fonɪ] (*phoney*) and puts him out of the game. In this scoring system, [fonɪ] represents a corruption of the word *phonetics*. Of course, any word will serve the same purpose.

After each demerit, the next player in turn begins a new sound sequence. The game continues until all but one of the players have been eliminated. The remaining player is the winner of the game. A word to the wise: When you indulge in this indoor or outdoor sport, the presence of a phonetic dictionary will smooth many ruffled tempers. Various restrictions might be desirable, such as prohibiting the use of proper names and foreign words. Groups with special interests might want to restrict the game to key words in titles of plays, novels, or songs. A little experimentation will quickly reveal the abilities or potentialities of your group of players.

Word Game 2

A geography game can also be played in phonetics. In this test of phonetic and geographic skill, the object is for each successive player to add a phoneme to those supplied in turn by the preceding players, which will further the sounding out of the name of a city or state. The last sound of each city or state so spelled (phonetically) serves as the initial sound of another city or state. Players drop out of the game when they are unable to add a sound, or when they are unable to supply a legitimate city or state name if challenged by the person who follows them. If a challenge is successfully met, the challenger must drop out of the game. The winner is the one person remaining after all others have dropped because of inability to meet a challenge or add an acceptable sound to those preceding. Variations of this game utilize the names of rivers, mountains, lakes, and so forth.

CROSSWORD PUZZLE WORD LIST

The first number after each word refers to the puzzle number. The second number and letter refer to the square in the puzzle, *a* meaning *across* and *d* meaning *down*.

Abel 4, 14a	an 3, 48d	auger 1, 38a
absolute 4, 45a	anarchy 1, 16d	aught 10, 33d
ace 3, 8d	anew 4, 46d; 5, 27d	aura 10, 15a
ache 4, 14d	anise 2, 7a	awed 1, 37a
aches 7, 35d	Anna 6, 36d	axe 3, 17d
acme 6, 18d; 10, 4a	annoy 1, 3d	
ad 2, 32d	annoyed 7, 15a	
add 3, 41d	annum 1, 16a	*b* 2, 60d
adjourn 5, 30a	ape 6, 29a; 7, 3d	baa 2, 38a
ado 6, 30a	apes 4, 36d; 10, 27d	back 7, 19d
a foe 5, 2d	appear 10, 3d	barge 2, 60a
agate 6, 19d	apple 2, 32a	bassoon 4, 43a
age 3, 33a	apt 8, 13a	bat 9, 31d
aid 7, 25a	are 2, 40a	bay 2, 14a
aim 3, 33d	arid 2, 39d	be 11, 27d
ain't 2, 15d	armistice 11, 10d	beach 7, 19a
airy 1, 5d	armor 11, 24a	beard 2, 17d
aisle 7, 37d	arrive 8, 21a	beast 2, 14d
Al 2, 7d	arrow 5, 18a	bellow 4, 16a
ale 6, 29d	art 11, 24d	bet 1, 4a
Alice 5, 31a	Art 4, 44a	biff 1, 4d
all 5, 20a	as 9, 22a	bird 9, 5d
alley 8, 24d	ash 3, 1d	birth 9, 31a
alleys 3, 17a	assay 5, 3d	blockades 7, 8d
ally (noun) 4, 55a	aster 11, 6a	blow 6, 39a
ally (verb) 1, 20d	at 3, 1a; 8, 24a	bode 2, 38d
am 4, 6d	ate 2, 19a	boil 9, 26a

honest 3, 28a
hood 9, 14a
howl 2, 5a

i 11, 2d
ichthy- 1, 29a
id 3, 44a
I'd 6, 26d
idling 4, 56a
idly 3, 38d
if 8, 38a
Ike 10, 25a
ill 4, 11d
I'll 9, 2d
I'm 10, 24d
immense 3, 30d
immerse 2, 9d
imp 10, 18a
in 8, 33a
inch 10, 31d
inches 10, 7d
inner 1, 31d
innervate 8, 17d
ion 2, 56d; 8, 9a
iotas 10, 1d
irate 2, 2d
ire 2, 51a
irk 10, 35d
isle 10, 25d
it 6, 12d
itch 6, 5d
itcher 6, 27a
item 10, 1a
its 10, 31a
ivory 2, 51d
ivy 1, 13a; 2, 56a

j 2, 58d
jaw 8, 11d
jazz 9, 28a
Jello 2, 26d
jerk 9, 28d
Jew 5, 22a
Jews 11, 16a
jive 8, 19d
joke 4, 30a
joy 1, 12a

k 8, 8a
knee 3, 51d
knife 9, 29d
knives 8, 10d

l 3, 46a
lake 1, 36a
lame 7, 31a
lamp 2, 12a
lash 8, 27d
launch 4, 28a
law 2, 33d
lead (verb) 4, 47d
leer 3, 11a
Lenin 7, 10d
let's 4, 10d
lettered 3, 18d
lie 6, 25a
lied 9, 7d
lightning 4, 33d
lime 3, 37a
lip 2, 21a
loafs 4, 27d
lobe 4, 35d
loose 2, 3d
lose 11, 4d
louse 5, 21a
love 6, 38d
luck 7, 31d
lunar 10, 9a
lute 8, 30a

m 11, 29d
ma 3, 49d
mace 9, 37d
mask 2, 20d
Massachusetts 5,   8d
mate 8, 32a
math. 9, 25d
May 9, 25a
mean 2, 20a
Mendel 10, 28a
met 9, 37a
Milwaukee 6, 24a
moo 4, 13a
moon 10, 6d
muse 11, 3d

nag 2, 8d
name 11, 32a
Navaho 6, 41a
nay 2, 59d
near 8, 35d
nearer 2, 48d
Negro 7, 7d
Nevada 6, 42a
New Mexico 5,32a

New York 6, 17d
niece 4, 51a
ninth 1, 8d
Noah 7, 41a
nod 3, 24d
node 1, 8a
nohow 3, 29d
noise 9, 23d
nook 9, 23a
nose 9, 29a

oak 3, 36d
oat 11, 20a
oath 4, 3d
oats 6, 2d
obey 1, 28d
oboe 1, 32a
occur 8, 3d
octagon 7, 1d
odd 11, 10a
odor 1, 34d
off 5, 6a
oil 4, 52d
O.K. 6, 23d; 7, 21a
olive 2, 40d
omen 11, 23d
on 2, 47a; 7, 22a
one 1, 35a
ooze 6, 31d; 11, 13a
opera 2, 28d
orchestral 3, 3a
Osage 4, 17d
ostrich 6, 9a
ouch 2, 6d
out 3, 32a
outs 6, 14a
ova 1, 9d
oven 1, 1a
over 1, 22a
owed 2, 4d
own 2, 37a; 6, 40d
owner 11, 20d

parts 2, 42d
pastry 10, 36a
paunch 10, 13a
paw 10, 32a
peach 9, 46a
peanut 7, 16d
peat 9, 13d
peerage 3, 14d
photostats 4, 2a

urge **9,** 6d
urn **1,** 7a
us **3,** 50d
use (noun) **4,** 39d
use (verb) **11,** 9a
ushered **1,** 39a

v **8,** 28a
vaccines **3,** 53a
vanish **7,** 23a
Vaseline **8,** 25a
vast **8,** 22d
vat **9,** 30d
veer **1,** 19d
verge **1,** 2d

verse **9,** 30a
vie **10,** 23a
vim **7,** 23d
voice **9,** 39d
vow **9,** 39a

wage **9,** 48a
wallow **5,** 11d
wane **9,** 41a
wash **1,** 33d
what **9,** 27a
whirs **9,** 27d
win **9,** 41d
witch **6,** 21d
woe **1,** 33a
wool **9,** 11d

wreck **9,** 33d
wren **9,** 3a

y **9,** 11a
yacht **9,** 20d
yawn **9,** 20a
yogi **6,** 22a
youth **4,** 32a

z **10,** 19a
Zack **6,** 35a
zebra **7,** 27d
Zeke **6,** 32a
Zeus **6,** 13a
zoo **8,** 12d

chapter 9

THE DYNAMICS OF SPEECH SOUNDS IN CONTEXT

Syllabic and phrasal stress
Unstressing
Regressive, progressive, and reciprocal assimilation
Complete and incomplete assimilation
Assimilated nasality
Dissimilation
Pitch phonemes
Punctuation
Selected reading passages

Syllabic and Phrasal Stress

By this time you should be consulting a phonetic dictionary regularly. If you are, you know that in phonetic transcription the prominent syllable[1] in a poly-syllabic word is indicated by a stress mark ['] *before* the syllable and above the line of writing, rather than by a heavy stress mark *after* the prominent syllable, as in standard dictionaries. Stress marks in phonetics are straight vertical lines rather than slanting ones. You may also have noted that some polysyllabic words contain syllables of a relatively medium degree of prominence—they are more prominent than one or more of the other syllables, yet less prominent than the syllable of greatest prominence. This type of stress may be designated by the secondary stress mark [ˌ], which precedes the syllable so stressed and appears below the line of writing. The standard nonphonetic dictionaries show secondary stress by a light stress mark *after* the syllable. Compare the phonetic dictionary's entry [ˌspɛkjə'leʃən] with the standard dictionary's spec'u la'tion. Syllables

1. The prominent syllable is usually the one which sounds loudest. In addition to intensity, the factors of duration and pitch also contribute in a complex manner to the prominence of a syllable, as previously noted on page 60. Additional optional notations for duration, quality, and pitch are presented later in this chapter.

containing unaccented vowels (those with minimal stress or prominence) appear without any qualifying mark.[2]

EXERCISE 67

A. Transcribe the following words, including stress marks:

1. college _____
2. kingdom _____
3. bastille _____
4. anger _____
5. conduct _____
6. devoid _____
7. capture _____
8. Netherlands _____
9. celluloid _____
10. Allies _____
11. shrivel _____
12. research _____
13. tureen _____
14. primeval _____
15. annex _____
16. beseech _____
17. pylon _____
18. unction _____

B. Circle the words above in which the stress mark is unnecessary. Why is it unnecessary?

EXERCISE 67: DISCUSSION

You should have circled *Allies* and *research* if you pronounce them [əlaɪz] and [rɪsɝtʃ]. If you pronounce them ['ælaɪz] and ['rɪsɝtʃ], however, they need stress marks. All four of these pronunciations are acceptable. These words remain in a state of flux with respect to the position of the stress. Where did you put the stress marks in *conduct* and *annex*? If you considered any alternatives for these two, it was probably on the basis of differentiating the part of speech intended. The next exercise should increase your sensitivity to these differences of emphasis.

---

2. Some phoneticians prefer to recognize four distinctive degrees of stress—primary ['], secondary [ˆ], tertiary [ˋ], and weak [˘]. The reader wishing to pursue this topic further should see Trager and Smith (1951, pp. 37-39). Since present dictionaries, including phonetic dictionaries, have no special mark for the fourth degree of stress—which is a pronunciation feature only when words are used in sentences—this book will not seek to make the subtle distinctions implied by the fourth degree (designated secondary [ˆ] in Trager and Smith).

EXERCISE 68

A. Transcribe each of the Column A words twice—in Column B as a noun and in Column C as a verb:

A	B (noun)	C (verb)
1. record	_____	_____
2. caution	_____	_____
3. confines	_____	_____
4. present	_____	_____
5. polish	_____	_____
6. increase	_____	_____
7. inlay	_____	_____
8. digest	_____	_____
9. insult	_____	_____
10. countermand	_____	_____
11. compress	_____	_____
12. extract	_____	_____

B. Circle the words in Column A above which are pronounced the same whether used as nouns or as verbs.

EXERCISE 68: DISCUSSION

You should have circled two words in Column A. Underscore the words in which the change from Column B to Column C was solely one of stress, the vowel sounds remaining unaffected. In these words we say the stress level alone has *distinctive value*. In most word pairs of this type the primary stress is on the first syllable in the noun form and on the second syllable in the verb form.

Just as we perceive varying degrees of *syllabic stress* in individual polysyllabic words, so we recognize *phrasal stress* in groups of words. The use of stress marks and of unstressed symbols follows the same rules whether we consider single words or groups of words; for example, compare the word [ˌɪnfləˈmeʃən] and the phrase [ˌɪn ðə ˈtɑnslz].

Unstressing

One of the trademarks of spoken English is the matter of unstressing. In English, much more than in most other languages, the unstressed sounds must have *very* little stress. The net effect is a great preponderance of schwa [ə] sounds, since in unstressing the vowel frequently migrates either to [ɪ] or to an indefinite vowel, the so-called neutral vowel, or schwa [ə]. This vowel shift is completely acceptable. In fact, insistence on stressed forms in unstressed syllables can result in affected speech.

Although many of us may never have consciously deliberated about phrasal and syllabic stress, most of us have been acutely aware of something wrong with the speech of a foreigner speaking English with an unfamiliar stress pattern. Frequently the problem lies in the speaker's careful, precise utterance of each syllable. To speak better English, he must observe unstressing – that is, he must say the unstressed syllables with less force and precision.

Earlier in this book you were told to transcribe all one-syllable words, except for the small filler words, such as *of*, *the*, and *a*, with an accented symbol *for the time being*. Actually, in phrasal context many one-syllable articles, auxiliary verbs, conjunctions, prepositions, and pronouns become unstressed and are transcribed accordingly. Now that the full complement of segmental phonemes has been studied, it is easier to move from the idea of syllabic stress to the larger sequences of phrasal stress.

In the phrase [ɪn ðə tɑnslz] above, *the* is transcribed with the schwa to indicate that in the process of vocal phrasing the vowel in *the* became the unstressed neutral vowel sound. However, the following transcriptions are also correct:

[ɪn ðɪ ist]	[ɪn ðə ʃɑp]
[ɑn ðə wɔl]	[əv ðɪ ɔrɪənt]
[əv ðɪ endʒəl]	[ɑn ðə mæntl̩]
[ɪn ðə gruv]	[ɑn ðɪ ɑnɪks mæntl̩]

Can you detect any pattern in the seemingly inconsistent transcription of *the* in the above eight examples? These examples should help you formulate a rule[3] for the transcription of *the*. Write the rule in this space:

_____

_____

_____

3. The rule formulated from these examples will usually not apply in the South, where [ðə] may be used in all contexts.

A similar rule (or set of related rules) could be formulated for the use of the indefinite article by studying the following examples:

[aɪ hæv ə bʊk]   [aɪ hæd n̩ ɑlɪv]

[aɪ hæv ən æpl̩]   [aɪ et n̩ æpl̩]

[aɪ bɔt ə bot]   [aɪ et ə pɛr]

[aɪ bɔt n̩ əlummnəm bot]   [aɪ kɔt ə frɪʃ]

Can you formulate rules which would encompass all of the above examples? Write them in the space below:

_____

_____

_____

_____

Variation in sound energy, or *intensity*, is one of the most important means of emphasis for effective speaking. By singling out a certain word in a phrase and saying it with greater force than the surrounding words, we can convey various emotional attitudes or degrees of meaning. In turn, the acoustic pattern helps the listener establish meaningful relationships among words. In this context let us take a look at our rules for stressing the small filler words.

When a normally unstressed vowel is stressed, we achieve a different meaning. Greater force of utterance for the second word in the sentence [nɑt ðʌ dʒɑn smɪθ?] clearly implies a *certain* person, and only one person. The word *the*, because of its loudness level, is the most prominent word in the sentence. Hence we transcribe it with the stressed symbol [ʌ] to indicate one *specific* person. Before nouns beginning with vowel sounds, we transcribe [ði] rather than [ðɪ] for emphasis, as in [ði æpl̩ wəz itn̩ baɪ snohwaɪt]. Here [ði] clearly designates one specific apple out of the legion of possible apples. Similarly, the indefinite article *a* in "I'll take *a* book" (meaning "not two") is transcribed with the stressed form [e] rather than the more usual unstressed [ə].

Obviously the intent of the speaker will change the stress of words as they are combined to form sentences. Thus, a complete study of stress would necessarily lead to the study of interpretation as well as of grammar.

If you understood the preceding material on the use of the definite and indefinite articles, you are ready for more involved decisions on the unstressing of other words. Just as the [i] and [ʌ] become [ɪ] and [ə] when unstressed, the [u] becomes [ʊ] or [ə] when unstressed. *And* frequently becomes [n̩], [ən], and sometimes [n̩d]. This pattern of unstressing also leads to acceptable vowel weakening or vowel shifts in words such as *an, as, from, of,* and *or.*

The following exercises should help you recognize more of these vowel shifts. Remember, always do these exercises *aloud*.

EXERCISE 69

Transcribe the indicated word as it would be said in reasonably rapid speech:

Pronoun

he 1. [wɪl _____ 'wɪn]

2. [_____ 'wɪl go]

3. [' _____ wɪl go]

4. [dɪd _____ 'go]

5. [_____ 'mʌst wɪn]

6. [' _____ mʌst wɪn]

7. [ɪz _____ 'ðɛr]

8. [ɪz ' _____ ðɛr]

you 1. [kæn _____ 'ɔfɚ ɪt]

2. [kæn ' _____ du ɪt]

3. [kæn _____ 'du ɪt]

4. [wɪl _____ ækt 'kwɪklɪ]

5. [wɪl _____ go 'sun]

6. [wɪl ' _____ go ɔr wɪl 'hi]

7. [_____ wɛnt 'ðɛr]

8. [' _____ wɛnt ðɛr]

her 1. [ʃɪ 'sod _____ drɛs]

2. [aɪ 'gev _____ maɪ ænsɚ]

3. [aɪ rest _____ hom]

4. [aɪ lʌv _____ 'mædlɪ]

5. [ɪz 'ðɪs _____ bʊk]

6. [ɪz ðɪs '_____ bʊk]

his   1. [hɪ 'dɪd _____ dænts]

2. [hɪ 'dʌg _____ gɑrdn̩]

3. ['græb _____ gʌn]

him   1. ['ʃo ɪt tʊ _____]

2. [kip _____ 'hɪr]

them   1. [aɪ 'hɝd _____ go]

Verbs

are   1. [hwɛr '_____ jʊ goɪŋ]

2. ['hwɛr _____ jʊ goɪŋ]

3. [hu _____ 'ju]

4. [hu '_____ ju]

were   1. ['hwɛr _____ ðə]

2. [hwɛr '_____ ðə]

3. [ðe _____ 'hɪr]

4. [_____ 'ðe hɪr]

can   1. [aɪ '_____ go]

2. [aɪ _____ 'go]

3. [hɪ '_____ du ɪt]

4. [' hi _____ du ɪt]

have, 1. [aɪ _____ 'gɔn]
has
2. [hi _____ 'gɔn]

3. [aɪ _____ 'itn̩ ɪt]

4. [' _____ ju itn̩ ɪt]

was 1. [aɪ _____ 'ðɛr]

2. [aɪ '_____ ðɛr]

3. [_____ ɪ 'ðɛr]

4. [hi '_____ ðɛr]

must 1. [wi '_____ du ɪt]

2. [wi _____ 'du ɪt]

Adverbs and Conjunctions

as 1. [ɪts _____ 'gʊd _____ dʌn]

2. [plæstɪk _____ strɔŋ _____ 'stil]

and 1. [hi _____ aɪ ɑr goɪŋ]

2. [ðə titɚtatɚ goz ʌp _____ daun]

3. [ðe wɛnt ʌp _____ bæk]

4. [θri _____ et ikwəlz tɛn]

5. [wek ʌp _____ sɪŋ]

6. [hæm _____ ɛgz]

7. [fɪʃ _____ faul]

8. [kæp _____ gaʊn]

or 1. [aɪl tek faɪv _____ sɪks]

2. [hi sɛd naɪn _____ et]

that 1. [mek 'ʃʊr _____ hi dʌz ɪt]

2. ['_____ ɪz ðə we]

Prepositions

to, 1. [aɪ 'hæv _____ kʌm]

two 2. [aɪ wɪʃ _____ 'go]

3. [hi 'kem _____ ʌs]

4. ju hæv frəm naʊ _____ eprɪl]

5. [dʒun _____ dʒulaɪ]

6. [aɪl wɝk frəm 'wʌn _____ 'θri]

7. [dɪd ju se '_____ ɚ 'θri]

for 1. [hi 'ped _____ ðə buk]

2. ['wet _____ mi]

3. [wet _____ ðə 'tren]

4. [tek wʌn _____ ðə 'rod]

from 1. [tek ɪt _____ 'mi]

2. [hiz 'hom _____ wɝk]

3. [hu ɪz ɪt '_____]

4. [ɪts _____ 'dʒæk]

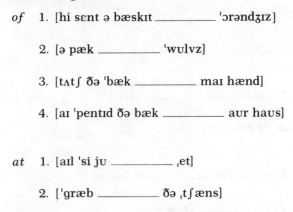

of   1. [hi sɛnt ə bæskɪt _____ 'ɔrəndʒɪz]

2. [ə pæk _____ 'wʊlvz]

3. [tʌtʃ ðə 'bæk _____ maɪ hænd]

4. [aɪ 'pentɪd ðə bæk _____ aʊr haʊs]

at   1. [aɪl 'si jʊ _____ ˌet]

2. ['græb _____ ðə ˌtʃæns]

The preceding exercise should help alert you to the effect of unstressing on phonetic transcription in running context. We note how the vowel sounds change in certain articles, conjunctions, prepositions, pronouns, verbs, and adverbs. We also note how words such as *and* and *him* can be reduced to syllabics in phrases such as [kip m̩ hɪr] and [hi n̩ aɪ]. Similarly *will*, when uttered as a contraction, becomes a syllabic [l̩], as in [ɪt̩ bɪ dʌn]. Check your answers with those of your classmates. Consult your teacher on transcriptions on which there are major disagreements.

Assimilation

Earlier in this book, when the [ŋ] sound was presented, you were left with the problem of determining why words such as *think* are pronounced with an [ŋ] rather than an [n]. You probably concluded correctly that the production of the following [k] sound demanded a tongue position which was too difficult to achieve rapidly from the [n] tongue position. Following an *economy of effort* principle, the tongue closure for the *n* is made farther back than that normally producing the [n] sound, so that the velar plosive [k] can be more easily produced. The resultant nasal sound is, of course, [ŋ]. This change in the production of a sound due to the manner of producing a neighboring sound is called *assimilation*. It is a principle that you first encountered on page 69.

There are three types of assimilation – regressive, progressive, and reciprocal – based on whether the sound production influences the manner of producing the *preceding* sound, the *following* sound, or *both*. The word *think*, in which the production of [k] influences the manner of producing the preceding sound, is an example of *regressive assimilation*. The rapid tongue movements necessary to move quickly from [n] to [k] are too difficult; therefore the tongue accommodates itself by making a contact farther back and an [ŋ] is produced in anticipation of the [k]. Similarly, the unvoiced character of the initial sound in *paper* tends to be anticipated in the combination word *newspaper*. This regressive assimilation results in unvoicing the [z], and the word is frequently pronounced [nuspepɚ]. Acceptance of the pronunciation [kəntrolɚ] for *comptroller* is an example of the influence of the alveolar [t] on the preceding bilabial sounds. However, an analogous example of regressive assimilation, [pʌŋkm] for *pumpkin,* is far more controversial when discussing acceptable pronunciations. (See Kenyon and Knott, 1949, p. 346.)

In phrases, as in individual words, the anticipated neuromuscular demands of an approaching sound can influence the manner of producing the immediately preceding sound. In the normal conversational flow of speech we would not say [ðɪs ʃʌvl̩ ɪz mam]. Instead, the voicing of the anticipated [ʃ] sound moves forward to the [s] and the two sounds become one elongated [ʃ]. To designate the distinctive function of the elongation, we use the symbol [ː][4] and transcribe the sentence [ðɪʃːʌvl̩ ɪz mam].

This type of assimilation, in which one sound is completely absorbed or changed into an adjacent sound, is called *complete assimilation.* The previously discussed assimilation of [n] into [ŋ] is an example of *partial* or *incomplete assimilation,* since the sound's production changed in the direction of, or became similar to, the production of its neighboring sound. However, although these two examples of assimilation – [ðɪʃːʌvl̩] and [θɪŋk] – differ in degree, they are both examples of regressive assimilation.

When identical consonants appearing adjacent to each other in separate syllables are linked or blended into one longer sound, we follow a single consonant phoneme with the mark of elongation [ː] – examples of this are found in [ðɪsːit], [kwɪkːɪk] and [tekːɑrl]. When the adjacent consonants are the voiced-voiceless cognates, neither sound can be said to *completely* disappear. For example, in *that day,* although only one stop-release occurs, the pressure build-up time is unvoiced, while the explosion is voiced. Hence the appropriate transcription would be [ðæt de].

EXERCISE 70

In these examples of regressive assimilation previously cited, check the appropriate column to show whether they are examples of *complete* or *incomplete* assimilation:

	Complete	Incomplete
1. [nuspepɚ]	_____	_____
2. [kəntrolɚ]	_____	_____
3. [pʌŋkm]	_____	_____

---

4. The mark of elongation is also used in this book to indicate the phonemic significance of a sound's lengthening such as that due to the deletion of a postvocalic [r]; for example, [hɑːt] for *heart,* [kɑːd] for *card,* and [bɑːn] for *barn.* The phonemic significance of the [ː] in Southern speech can be appreciated particularly by studying the contrasting vowel lengths in the following word pairs: *hod* [hɑd]–*hard* [hɑːd], *pot* [pɑt]–*part* [pɑːt], and *lock* [lɑk]–*lark* [lɑːk]. Aside from a limited number of examples of this type, elongation does not serve as a distinctive feature in American English speech.

Progressive assimilation occurs when the manner of one sound's production influences the way in which the following sound is produced. Thus, the voicing of the [b] in *absorption* causes the ensuing [s] to change to the voiced form [z], making the word [æb'zɔrpʃən]. Progressive assimilation is not so frequent a phenomenon as regressive assimilation.

EXERCISE 71

Read each of the following statements for accuracy. Record [j] (yes) if the final word is correctly transcribed and [n] (no) if it is incorrectly transcribed:

_____ 1. [ðə plurəl əv ɛg ɪz ɛgs]

_____ 2. [ðə plurəl əv bɛt ɪz bɛts]

_____ 3. [ðə plurəl əv bɛd ɪz bɛds]

_____ 4. [ðə plurəl əv fɛns ɪz fɛnsɪs]

_____ 5. [ðə plurəl əv prɪns ɪz prɪnsɪs]

_____ 6. [ðə plurəl əv kalɪdʒ ɪz kalɪdʒɪz]

_____ 7. [ðə plurəl əv laɪbrɛrɪ ɪz laɪbrɛrɪs]

_____ 8. [ðə plurəl əv flis ɪz flisɪz]

_____ 9. [ðə plurəl əv flaɪ ɪz flaɪs]

_____ 10. [ðə plurəl əv bɝd ɪz bɝdz]

_____ 11. [ðə plurəl əv klæʃ ɪz klæʃɪz]

_____ 12. [ðə plurəl əv pɝs ɪz pɝsɪz]

_____ 13. [ðə plurəl əv plɔɪ ɪz plɔɪs]

_____ 14. [ðə plurəl əv θɪŋ ɪz θɪŋz]

_____ 15. [ðə plurəl əv grev ɪz grevs]

_____ 16. [ðə plurəl əv bʌg ɪz bʌgs]

_____ 17. [ðə plurəl əv tʃɝtʃ ɪz tʃɝtʃɪz]

_____ 18. [ðə plurəl əv batl̩ ɪz batl̩s]

_____ 19. [ðə plurəl əv bitʃ ɪz bitʃɪz]

_____ 20. [ðə plurəl əv kwɝk ɪz kwɝks]

EXERCISE 72

Read each of the following statements for accuracy. Write [j] if the final word is correctly transcribed and [n] if it is incorrectly transcribed:

_____ 1. [ðə pæst:ɛns əv wɔk ɪz wɔkt]

_____ 2. [ðə pæst:ɛns əv rʌb ɪz rʌbd]

_____ 3. [ðə pæst:ɛns əv wɑnt ɪz wɑntɪd]

_____ 4. [ðə pæst:ɛns əv skwɛr ɪz skwɛrd]

_____ 5. [ðə pæst:ɛns əv hauz ɪz hauzd]

_____ 6. [ðə pæst:ɛns əv tɔs ɪz tɔsd]

_____ 7. [ðə pæst:ɛns əv hʌnt ɪz hʌntɪd]

_____ 8. [ðə pæst:ɛns əv rɪp ɪz rɪpd]

_____ 9. [ðə pæst:ɛns əv puʃ ɪz puʃd]

_____ 10. [ðə pæst:ɛns əv beð ɪz beðd]

_____ 11. [ðə pæst:ɛns əv kraɪ ɪz kraɪd]

_____ 12. [ðə pæst:ɛns əv læf ɪz læfd]

_____ 13. [ðə pæst:ɛns əv wɔk ɪz wɔkd]

_____ 14. [ðə pæst:ɛns əv switʃ ɪz switʃd]

_____ 15. [ðə pæst:ɛns əv plau ɪz plaud]

_____ 16. [ðə pæst:ɛns əv kɪk ɪz kɪkd]

_____ 17. [ðə pæst:ɛns əv fes ɪz fesd]

_____ 18. [ðə pæst:ɛns əv lɪŋk ɪz lɪŋkd]

_____ 19. [ðə pæst:ɛns əv ɪvok ɪz ɪvokd]

_____ 20. [ðə pæst:ɛns əv ku ɪz kud]

EXERCISE 71 and EXERCISE 72: DISCUSSION

In each of the two preceding exercises you should have recorded ten [n]'s and ten [j]'s. In checking over your answers, study these two exercises carefully to see what principles are illustrated.

EXERCISE 73

In the space below, write rules that would apply to the problems illustrated by the nouns and verbs in Exercises 71 and 72:

_____

_____

_____

_____

_____

_____

Compare what you have just written with the following explanations. The unvoiced final [s] sound of the verb *race* affects the pronunciation of the past tense by changing the [d] of *raced* to an unvoiced [t] sound [rest]. Similarly the past tense or past participle of other verb roots ending with an unvoiced sound other than [t] are formed by adding the [t] sound. When the verb root ends in a voiced sound other than [d], the inflectional ending is pronounced with the voiced [d], as in *lived* [lɪvd]. If the root of the verb ends in the [t] or [d] sound, another syllable is added in forming the past tense, as in *wanted* [wɑntɪd]; the addition of the vowel sound [ɪ] or [ə] causes the final consonant of the inflectional ending to be voiced.

Just as the process of progressive assimilation enables us to formulate a rule about the voicing or unvoicing of inflectional -*ed* endings of verbs, so this process also enables us to formulate a rule about the voicing or unvoicing of the plural or possessive forms of nouns. If the plural or possessive is formed without adding another syllable, the voiced [z] is added to nouns ending in voiced sounds, while the voiceless [s] is added to nouns ending in voiceless consonant sounds. For example, [lɪd] becomes [lɪdz], whereas [hæt] becomes [hæts]. When the singular form ends in [s], [z], [ʃ], [ʒ], [tʃ], or [dʒ], another syllable, formed by [ɪz] or [əz], is necessary to indicate the plural. In this case, the voicing of the vowel sound in the inflectional ending is carried over, making the final consonant sound the voiced [z], as in [res] – [resɪz].

The preceding rule for [s] and [z] endings also holds for the pronunciation of the third person singular form of verbs. Thus, the final voicing of *turns* [tɝnz] contrasts with the voiceless ending of *sits* [sɪts].

The assimilation of voicing can also be noticed intervocally in *Lady Betty,* the brand name of a product advertised in some parts of the country. Radio and television announcers consistently demonstrate little or no difference in the second consonant sounds of these two words. Phoneticians have a way of transcribing the voicing of the [t] in *Betty.* As noted on page 27, a little *v* is placed under the sound to indicate that the normally unvoiced sound is made with voicing – [bɛtɪ]. Another common example is the phrase [hwəts ðə mætɚ]. As noted on page 30, another mark is used to show that a sound which is usually voiced is made without voicing. In this case a little zero, or circle, is placed under the symbol, for example, [sigəlz]. This modifying mark can also be used under vowels to indicate whispering.

The example [ledɪ bɛdɪ] brings to mind another problem sometimes encountered by speech correctionists and by teachers of voice and diction. In certain persons, greatly enlarged tonsillar and adenoidal tissue blocks the pharyngeal opening into the nasal cavities, prohibiting the production of the nasal resonance necessary for [m] and [n]. Thus, these people would say [bɛdɪ ɛbɪdəd wɪbɪd] for the phrase *many eminent women.*

Reciprocal assimilation is a combination of both progressive and regressive assimilation. Two adjacent sounds affect each other to such an extent that they both disappear and a third sound emerges in their place. Thus, in the evolution of the pronunciation of the word *nation,* the sounds for *t* and *i* have been replaced by the [ʃ] sound. A word currently in the process of changing in this way is *maturation,* for which both [mætjureʃən] and [mætʃureʃən] are acceptable. This word is an example of pronunciation in a state of transition (in this case, from the two sounds [t] and [j] to the affricate [tʃ]).

This short treatment of types of assimilation might be summarized by saying that sounds may be changed, added, or eliminated because of the difficulty of the extent or rapidity of movement demanded of the lips, jaws, tongue, or velum in producing certain sound sequences. No doubt there are certain sound combinations which cause you articulatory difficulty. Many persons remember a long period of conscious effort spent in mastering the articulation of such words as *soothsayer, fifth,* and *statistics.* It is difficult to predict which current mispronunciations of similar words might be acceptable pronunciations a decade or two from now. With the passage of time, the forces of assimilation will continue to affect standards of pronunciation. But our *best* criteria for *acceptable* pronunciation are the speech of well-educated persons and the reflection of this speech in our dictionaries.

While it is fascinating to study the sound changes that have occurred in our language in the past, this subject is the concern of *historical* or *diachronic linguistics,* and not a major concern of this book. The study of recent sound changes, or changes currently in progress, is part of the discipline known as *synchronic linguistics.*

Another type of assimilation which does not effect a distinctive difference in our language but which is esthetically very disturbing to some people is *assimi-lated nasality.* This term refers to the spread of nasalization from the nasal consonants [m], [n], and [ŋ] to the adjacent vowel sounds—for example, [hɪ dænst fɔr ɪz rænsôm]. Note that only the vowels adjacent to the nasal consonants are indicated as receiving nasality.

Dissimilation

Another type of sound change related to assimilation is *dissimilation.* This is the alteration of one of two identical or similar sounds in a word. As the name *dissimilation* suggests, the change is in the direction of making the production of the sounds *less* like each other. Many students use dissimilation daily when they say they are going to the [laɪbɛrɪ], thereby avoiding the repeated [r] sounds of [laɪbrɛrɪ]. Similarly (but more widely accepted), the first r sound in *surprise* [səpraɪz] is disappearing. We sometimes alter the *n − m* sequence in *government* by saying [gʌvɚmənt], although the *n − m* sequence is more generally retained in *environment.* Indeed, *government* seems particularly susceptible to change— note the frequent pronunciation of [gʌvənɚ] for [gʌvɚnɚ]. These four pronunci-ations illustrating the principle of dissimilation are gaining wider acceptance in this country.

Thus far in this chapter we have become aware of some of the forces that oper-ate when sounds and words are put together in meaningful speech. We have seen assimilation at work on both consonants and vowels. We have also noted some of the effects of stressing and unstressing on sound production. Now we need to look even more closely at the influence of adjacent phonemes upon each other.

Frequently in rapid speech no final explosion of breath is heard on the final [p], [t], or [k] sounds. You may recall that this is why we use the classification *stops* rather than *plosives.* A maple-syrup farmer talks about the *sack.* How can we tell whether he means *sack* or *sap* if the final stop sound is not exploded? The preparation for and movement to the place of closure required by the appro-priate consonant exert their influence upon the quality (see G. I.) of the preceding vowel. Thus, we recognize or "hear" the consonant because of the unique quality of the vowel which has been modified in preparing for the following consonant, even though the consonant may never be *sounded.*

A related phenomenon is the influence of vowels on preceding consonants. For example, the vowels [i] and [ɔ] following the [t] in *teak* and *talk* cause quite dissimilar sounding [t]'s. Here the [t] is influenced by the characteristics of the different vowels which follow.

Such influences of phonetic context on consonant sounds have far-reaching implications for the speech correctionist. Certainly they raise questions about the usefulness of drilling single consonant sounds in isolation. The person with an articulation problem needs to get the feel of the flow of speech. Hence phonetic contexts must be drilled. On this basis we can understand the value of the "nuclei words" which Van Riper (1954, p. 246) considers "veritable nuggets." These words, in which the usually misarticulated sound is articulated correctly, can yield insight into the phonetic contexts from which to begin corrective work. The influence of adjacent sounds also raises questions about the procedures used in articulation testing to ascertain which sounds are produced incorrectly. For example, in how many phonetic contexts must a consonant be tested in order to obtain valid test results?

Pitch Phonemes

The qualifying marks ['] and [ˌ] were introduced earlier in this book to designate degrees of stress. These symbols are called *suprasegmental elements* (see G. I.) in contrast to the specific sound symbols, or *segmental phonemes* (see G. I.), such as [i], [p], [tʃ], and [aʊ]. Other suprasegmental elements can be used to designate pitch functions.

The International Phonetic Association has recommended a system of pitch annotation (IPA, 1949) utilizing small diacritical marks. If pitch annotation is to be used, we prefer the greater readability of the four-degree pitch designation cited by Trager and Smith (1951, page 42), which has achieved fairly wide usage. In this system of pitch designation the pitch-level of normal monotone speech is designated [2]. The lowest level, or range of tones, is designated [1]; the higher levels are designated [3] and [4], with [4] indicating the highest pitch range. In phonetic transcription the pitch phonemes are placed above the line of writing of the vowel, consonant, and diphthong symbols. Upward, downward, and level inflection arrows are also used (Pike, 1945).

The relative importance of designating pitch phonemes is obviously based on the use to which students will put their knowledge of phonetics. The importance of *intonation* (see G. I.) in learning to speak and to read was affirmed in Donald Lloyd's talk on "Reading American English Sound Patterns" delivered to the Chicago Area Reading Association in May 1961. The growing importance of intonation in linguistic studies suggests an ever-increasing use of pitch phonemes.

Punctuation

[frikwəntlɪkɑlɪdʒstudn̩tsmedʒɚrɪŋɪnspitʃ | ɑrhɝdtuse | bʌθwaɪməstaɪstʌdɪfonɛtɪks]. Those of you who persevered through the preceding line of phonetics may have recognized it as a transcription of the first line of the preface to this book. This line of transcription illustrates some of the possible hazards of transcription in context. Words, as known to linguists and grammarians, usually do not possess individual sound autonomy within the flow of continuous discourse. If we were to represent faithfully (by blank spaces, or any type of arbitrary symbol) only the pauses that occurred, the result would be similar to that illustrated above. For practical purposes, and in accord with many other texts, in this book we generally reflect the word divisions of conventional orthography in the transcription passages. The traditional marks of punctuation, other than the apostrophe, are also used in transcription. The idea of combining two different notational systems might be criticized by a purist; nevertheless this procedure makes for easier reading.

Surely the following is easier to read than the above "blended" passage:

[ðə praɪmɛrɪ em əv ðɪs bʊk ɪs tə tren ju, ðə studn̩t, tʊ hɪr ðə soundz

əv əmɛrəkən spitʃ — pətɪkjələ⋅lɪ θoz ju jʊrsɛlf ʌtə⋅ — ænd tə trænscraɪb

ðiz saʊnds baɪ minz əv fənɛtɪk sɪmbl̩z. tu sɛkəndɛrɪ emz ɑr tə gɪv ju ən

ʌndə⋅stændɪŋ əv haʊ əmɛrəkən spitʃ saundz ə⋅ prədust æn tə prəvaɪd ju

wɪθ ən ɛləmɛntrɪ knɑlɪdʒ ʌv phonɛtɪʃ ənz tə⋅mənɑlədʒɪ ənd ɛrɪəz əv stʌdɪ.]

It is certainly to be hoped that the reader has detected mistakes in the preceding passage. An analysis of the mistakes may help sharpen your transcription abilities.

EXERCISE 74

Carefully review the preceding transcription passage as it might be read aloud by a Midwesterner using good standard speech. On this basis, circle each error you find.

EXERCISE 74: DISCUSSION

Compare your list of errors with the following analysis. The transcription contains:

1. Seven errors reflecting spellings rather than sounds.
2. Four substitutions of a voiceless symbol for its voiced cognate (two of which are also tallied in the 7 above).
3. One error of stress.
4. One instance of adjacent words in which the common stop ending the first word and beginning the second might be exploded only once.

Did any of these errors elude you? If so, do not be too disheartened if the ones you missed belonged to the first category of seven spelling similarities. Our reading and writing habits are so thoroughly ingrained that this kind of error could easily pass unnoticed. Failure to catch such an error would not necessarily suggest that you have not mastered either the hearing of sounds or the system of phonetic annotation. Now that you know that extreme precision and care are demanded, try another passage.

EXERCISE 75

Circle all transcription errors. Remember the old warning: *Sound out all the words!*

[ðə tɜ˞m fonɛtɪcs me bi dɪfined æs ðə scaɪəns of spitʃ soundz, ɔr əz ðə

saɪəntɪfɪc stʌdɪ əv spitʃ saunds frəm ðə stændpɔɪntz ʌv ðɛr prədʌkʃən,

rɪsɛpʃən, ænd sɪmbḷəzeʃən. fonɛtɪx ɪz ɔlso juzd tʊ dɛzɪgnet ðə symbḷz

juzd tʊ rɛprɪzɛnt spitʃ saundz vɪʒuəlɪ].

EXERCISE 75: DISCUSSION

This passage contains:

1. Ten words having errors reflecting spelling rather than sounds.
2. Three substitutions of a voiceless symbol for its voiced cognate (all of which are also tallied in the ten above).
3. One substitution of a voiced symbol for its voiceless cognate.
4. One error of stress.

Selected Reading Passages

EXERCISE 76

Read the following passage as rapidly as you can without losing the sense of the paragraph:

[ɪŋglɪʃ ɪz ə wʌndɚful:æŋgwɪdʒ æn ɪn sʌm rɪspɛkts əmɛrəkən ɪŋglɪʃ

me bɪ ivn̩ bɛtɚ. no ʌðɚ ɪz mɔr prɪsaɪs ænd, æt ðə sem taɪm mɔr flɛksəbḷ

ɔr mɔr:ɪspɑnsɪv tə nu nidz, n̩ ðæt ɪz bɪkɔz no ʌðɚ həz mɔr səksɛsfəlɪ

strʌk ə bæləns bətwin stəbɪlətɪ n̩ tʃendʒ. pɛdn̩ts n̩ pjurɪsts ɚ ɔlwɪz

traɪɪŋ tə friz ɪt ɪntʊ ə dɛd læŋgwɪdʒ laɪk "gʊd" lætn; ðə sɛmɪlɪtərɪt ɚ

ɔlwɪz tɛndɪŋ tə rɪdus ɪt:u ən ɪnkohɪrənt dʒɑrgən onlɪ rʌflɪ kɑmprɪhɛnsəbḷ

ivn̩ tə mɛmbɚz wɪðɪn ə smɔl grup. itʃ tɛndənsɪ həz kɛpt ðɪ ʌðɚ ɪn tʃɛk.

ɪf ðə naɪntinθ sɛntʃərɪ skulmarm əd hɛd hɚ we, ɪt wʊd bɪ dʒɛntɪl n̩ prɪsɪ;

ɪf ðɪ ɪlɪtərɪt əd hɛd ðɛr we, ɪt wʊd bɪ ə barbrəs dʒɑrgən].

— transcribed from Joseph Wood Krutch, "English As She Is Spoken,"
Saturday Review, July 4, 1959, p. 22.

EXERCISE 77

The following montage of gems from college freshman themes was assembled by Ralph S. Graber to suggest the effect of learning to speak through spoken rather than written language. Read the passage aloud and then write it out in English script on a separate sheet of paper:

[nau əv dez ıt ız kwaıt dıfəkəlt tə faımd ə studn̩t hu dʌzn̩t hæv ə dɛvl̩-meks-hɛr ætətjud n̩ tek hız ɛdʒəkeʃənl̩ apətjunəti fə grænıt. ðə studn̩t dʌz nat du hız ʌpmost ın hız stʌdız, nɔr dʌz hı pəzɛs ðə sɛlf-ınʃurəns nɛsəsɛrı fɔr ım tə fes ðə kəmplɛksıŋ prabləmz əv kalıdʒ].

—transcribed from *Time*, August 31, 1959, p. 34.

EXERCISE 78

Read the following passage as rapidly as you can without losing the sense of the paragraph:

[ði ıntənæʃənl̩ fənɛtık ælfəbɛt əz tu tʃif ədvæntıdʒız — ın ðə fɜ˞st ples ıt ız ði əfıʃəl ælfəbɛt əv ən əstæblıʃt badı əv skaləz n̩ ðʌs hæz bıhaımd ıt ðə wet əv prɛstiʒ n̩ skaləʃıp. sɛkəndlı, ıt ız mɔr waıdlı non ðən ɛnı ʌðə˞ sıstəm əv saund rɛprızenteʃən ıksɛpt ðə daıəkrıtıkl̩ markıŋz juzd ın ðə vɛriəs dıkʃənɛrız. ıt ız, əz ıt wə˞, ði ɛspəranto əv fonətıʃənz — hwıtʃ minz ðət ıt sɜ˞vz əz ðə bɛst əveləbl̩ midıəm fɔr ði ıkstʃendʒ əv aıdıəz ın ðıs prəfɛʃənl̩ fild].

—transcribed from Claude E. Kantner and Robert West, *Phonetics*, New York: Harper & Brothers, 1960, p. 311.

EXERCISE 79

Transcribe the following paragraphs on a sheet of paper as you believe you would say them in a conversational speaking manner:

For communication to take place, there must be both a source of the pressure variations which we call speech sounds, and a destination for these sound waves. The aim of the speaker, or source, is to elicit in his auditor, or receiver, meanings which correspond to those he himself holds.

Many factors are involved in the accuracy with which the speaker is able to convey his meaning to the audience, and hence the degree to which communication is effective. Teachers of public speaking have traditionally emphasized the importance of the communication abilities of the speaker, his familiarity with his subject, and his feelings toward his subject matter and toward his listeners, as factors which make his speech effective.

Recent trends in speech education have shown ever-increasing emphasis on pre-speaking analysis of the intended receiver of the spoken words. The speaker should take into consideration the receiver's own communication proficiency, his familiarity with the subject matter, and his attitudes and feelings toward both the subject matter and the speaker himself. The effectiveness of communication is further influenced by the social and cultural forces present in the setting in which the attempt to communicate occurs.

— above paragraphs based on ideas contained in David K. Berlo, *The Process of Communication*, New York: Holt, Rinehart and Winston, Inc., 1960.

EXERCISE 79: DISCUSSION

After completing your transcription of the preceding paragraphs, answer the following questions:

1. Paragraph 1, line 1: Why are you most apt to say [tʊ] for *to*? Why not [tu] or [tə]?
2. Paragraph 1, line 3: Explain your choice of vowels in the *the*'s which appear before *aim* and *speaker.*
3. Paragraph 1, line 4: How did you transcribe *or receiver*? Why?
4. Paragraph 2: Did you give different transcriptions for the three *and*'s in this paragraph? Why or why not?
5. Paragraph 3, line 1: How did you transcribe *Recent trends*? If you used two *t*'s, are you sure you would pronounce both?
6. Paragraph 3, line 8: Did you use a *t* to end *attempt* plus another to begin the following *to*? Why or why not?
7. Did any words cause you undue difficulty? If so, check with your dictionary or your teacher.

EXERCISE 80

Read the following passage aloud, assuming a normal conversational delivery. Circle those elements which you consider to be incorrectly transcribed:

[ə rɪtn̩ wɝd ɪz ðʌ tʃɔɪsɪst əv rɛlɪks. ɪt ɪz sʌmθɪŋ ət wʌns mɔr ɪntəmɪt

wɪð əs n̩d mɔr junəvɝsl̩ ðæn ɛnɪ əðɚ wɝk əv ɑrt. ɪt ɪz ðə wɝk əv ɑrt

nɪrɪst tu laɪf ɪtsɛlf. ɪt me bi trænsletɪd ɪntu ɛvrɪ læŋgwɪdʒ, n̩:at onlɪ bɪ

rɛd bət æktʃuəlɪ briðd frəm ɔl humən lɪps; — nɑt bɪ rɛprɪzɛntɪd ɑn kænvəs

ɚ ɪn mɑrbl̩ onlɪ, bət bɪ kɑrvd aut əv ðə brɛθ əv laɪf ɪtsɛlf].

— transcribed from Henry David Thoreau, *Walden*

EXERCISE 80: DISCUSSION

Aside from possible dialectical differences, you should have noted two errors in stress in the first sentence and another one in the following sentence. Did you eliminate the repeated [t] sound in sentence three? Did you notice that a [j] was missing in the word *human*? Check additional disagreements with your instructor.

EXERCISE 81

Be prepared to read aloud in class the following passage exactly as transcribed:

[wi sʌmtaɪmz faɪnd arsɛlvz tʃendʒɪŋ ar maɪndz wɪðaut ɛnɪ rɪzɪstəns

ɚ hɛvɪ ɪmoʃən, bət ɪf wi ɚ told ðət wi ɚ rɔŋ wi rɪzɛnt ðɪ ɪmpjuteʃən n̩d

hardn̩ ar harts. wi ɚ ɪnkrɛdəblɪ hidlɪs ɪn ðə fɔrmeʃən əv ar bɪlifs, bət

faɪnd aursɛlvz fɪld wɪð ən ɪlɪsɪt pæʃən fɔr ðəm hwɛn ɛnɪwən prəpozɪz

tə rɑb əs əv ðɛr kəmpænjənʃɪp. ɪt ɪz abvɪəslɪ nɑt ðɪ aɪdiəz ðɛmsɛlvz

ðət ar dɪr tu əs, bət ar sɛlf əstim, hwɪtʃ ɪz θrɛtn̩d . . . fju əv əs tek ðə penz

tə stʌdɪ ðɪ ɔrədʒən əv ar tʃerɪʃt kənvɪkʃənz; ɪndid, wi hæv ə nætʃrəl

rɪpʌgnəns tə so duɪŋ. wi laɪk tə kəntɪnju tə bəliv hwət wi hæv bɪn

əkʌstəmd tu æksɛpt əz tru, æn ðə rɪzɛntmənt ərauzd hwɛn daut ɪz kæst

əpɑn ɛnɪ əv ar əsʌmpʃənz lidz əs tə sik ɛvrɪ mænɚ əv ɪkskjus fɚ klɪŋɪŋ tə ðəm. ðə rızʌlt ız ðæt most əv ar sokɔld rizənıŋ kənsısts ın faındıŋ argjəmənts fɚ goıŋ an bılivıŋ əz wi ɔlrɛdı du].

—transcribed from James Harvey Robinson, *The Mind in the Making*, New York: Harper & Brothers, 1939, pp. 40-41.

EXERCISE 82

Read the following passage as rapidly as you can without losing the sense of the paragraph:

[ıf ju du nat æktʃuəlı laık bɔız ŋ̩ gɚlz, ɚ jʌŋ mɛn ən jʌŋ wımın, giv ʌp titʃıŋ. ıt ız izı tə laık ðə jʌŋ bıkʌz ðe ar jʌŋ. ðe hæv no fɔlts, ıksɛpt ðə vɛrı wʌnz hwıtʃ ðe ɚ æskıŋ ju tu ırædıket; ıgnərəns, ʃælonıs, n̩ ınıkspırıəns. ðə rılı hetfəl fɔlts ɚ ðoz hwıtʃ wi gron mɛn ən wımın hæv. sʌm əv ðiz gro an əs laık dızizız, ʌðɚz wi bıld ʌp n̩ tʃɛrıʃ əz ðo ðe wɚ vɚtʃuz. ıngrend kənsit, kælkjələtıd kruəltı, dip rutıd kauɚdıs, slabərıŋ grid, vʌlgɚ sɛlf sætısfækʃən, pʌfı lezınəs əv maınd n̩ badı—ðiz n̩ ðı ʌðɚ ril sınz rızʌlt frəm jirz, dɛkədz əv kɛrfəl kʌltəve ʃən. ðe ʃo an ar fesız, ðe rıŋ harʃ ɔr halo ın ar vɔısız; ðe həv bıkʌm bon əv ar bon ən flɛʃ əv ar flɛʃ. ðə jʌŋ du nat sın ın ðoz wez. hɛvən noz ðe ar ınfjurıetıŋlı lezı n̩ ənbəlivəblı stupıd n̩ sʌmtaımz dıtɛstəblı krud—bʌt nat fɚ lɔŋ, nat ɔl ət wʌns, n̩:at (laık gronʌps) əz ə mætɚ əv hæbıt ɔr paləsı. ðe ar traıŋ tə bı ɛnɚdʒɛtık ən waız ən kaınd. hwɛn ju rımɛmbɚ ðıs, ıt ız dıfəkəlt nat:u laık ðəm].

—transcribed from Gilbert Highet, *The Art of Teaching*, New York: Vintage Books, Inc., 1955, p. 25.

APPENDICES

RESPIRATION, PHONATION, AND RESONATION

Essential to the study of phonetics is an understanding of the speech mechanism and the relationship of articulation to the processes of *respiration, phonation,* and *resonation.* This Appendix presents in a brief and cursory fashion the anatomic and physiologic information basic to an introductory phonetics course. This material is a skeletal outline which should be supplemented by the instructor or by reading. A more detailed discussion is not possible here due to space considerations and the workbook aspect of this book.

The three essential components of the speech mechanism[1] are (1) a bellows system, or air pressure generator, (2) a system of sound sources, and (3) a resonant transmission system, or path of egress for the sound vibrations.

The bellows system: Respiration

The lungs and their tubular entry system, together with the chest cage and its related musculature, make up the bellows system. The flow of air in and out of the lungs is brought about by the continually changing relationship of the pressure of the outside atmosphere to that within the thoracic (chest) cavity.

Inhalation is the rushing in of air to equalize the partial vacuum or decrease in pressure created by enlargement of the thoracic cavity. The cavity becomes enlarged when cerebral controls stimulate nerve fibers which cause various thoracic muscles to contract, raising the entire rib cage. At the same time, the muscle fibers of the diaphragm—the muscular and tendonous floor of the thoracic cavity—contract, causing it to move downward. This action pushes the viscera out against the abdominal wall.

Exhalation occurs when the thoracic cavity diminishes in size, acting like a bellows and causing the compressed air to rush out. In general terms, exhalation is caused by the relaxation of the muscles used in inhalation, as well as the action of various abdominal muscles which bring the abdominal wall inward, compressing the viscera and forcing them, and thus the diaphragm and the base of the lungs, upward (see figure 9).

The basic biological purpose of this continual movement of air in and out of the lungs is to supply oxygen to the blood stream and to remove carbon dioxide from it. (This exchange of gases occurs within the lungs by means of osmosis— a diffusion through the semipermeable membranes which comprise the walls of the lungs' air sacs, or alveoli.) Respiration is regulated by automatic controls which help us meet varying biological demands. For speech, we change the

---

[1]This discussion is adapted from Curtis (Johnson et. al., 1956, pp. 162-163).

normal and relatively periodic intake and expulsion of air by shortening the inhalation phase and lengthening the exhalation phase of the breathing cycle. The antagonistic action of the abdominal exhalation muscles and the diaphragmatic and thoracic inhalation muscles helps sustain and control the outward flow of air as needed for speech. While the abdominal muscles are the primary source of the pressure necessary to sustain phrase-length breath groups, the pulses of air pressure which accompany each syllable are produced by certain muscles of the rib cage.

A system of sound sources: Phonation

Air moves out of the right and left lungs by means of two bronchial tubes which join to form the trachea, or windpipe. At the top of the trachea is the larynx, which functions as a valve between the pharynx (throat) and the trachea. The larynx, a tubular structure lying in front of the esophagus, is the organ of phonation. The anterior shieldlike portion, called the thyroid cartilage, is the structure which can be felt by placing the fingers on the midline of the front surface of the neck just below the chinline. This cartilage is particularly prominent when the head is tilted up and back.

Behind this cartilaginous shield are the vocal folds — two highly flexible structures of ligament and muscle covered by mucous membrane. They are attached at the sides to the inner walls of the larynx. The front ends of both

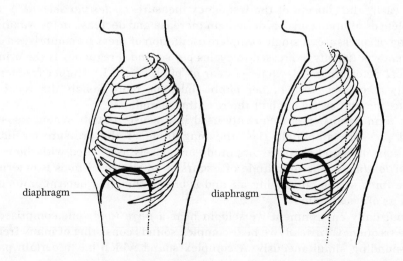

Fig. 9. The thoracic area during inhalation and exhalation.

folds are joined within the angle on the inner surface of the thyroid cartilage. The back ends of the folds attach to the lower front projections of two tiny pyramid-shaped cartilages called arytenoids. These cartilages are located on the upper surface of the back part of the cricoid cartilage, the rigid tubular top of the trachea. The actions of various laryngeal muscle groups alter certain cartilaginous relationships and enable multidirectional movements of the arytenoids, permitting opening and shutting, stretching and shortening, and tensing and relaxing of the vocal folds.

The term *glottis* is applied to the vocal folds themselves or to the triangular-shaped variable opening between them. During normal quiet respiration, the vocal folds lie at rest in an open position. To "close the larynx," the left and right vocal folds move toward each other in a horizontal direction.

The vocal folds serve as the generator of the periodic sound vibrations which we hear as *vocal tones*, or *voice*. When we speak, the tensed vocal folds are brought together by means of laryngeal muscles, and are rhythmically opened and closed by the rapidly changing subglottal (see G.I.) pressures of the outward rushing air stream. The vocal folds do not operate in a simple open-shut fashion; a very complex type of undulation accompanies the lateral movements of the cords. The complexity of this movement varies not only with pressure adjustments but also with the internal laryngeal adjustments which vary the frequency, intensity, and wave composition of the tone being produced. The rapidly alternating pressure changes which result from the vibration of the vocal cords (and which vary in rate from fifty or sixty per second to several hundred per second) are radiated into the air and transmitted to the ear, where they set our eardrums into vibration, enabling us to perceive what we call vocal sounds.

The pressure variations that we perceive as voice have three major dimensions, or attributes, in addition to the obvious dimension of time, or duration. These are *frequency*, *intensity*, and *wave composition*.

By viewing pressure variations as oscillations of pressure, we can visualize more easily the concept of the frequency measure, *cycles per second*. A single complete oscillation consists of both an increase and decrease in (or waxing and waning of) pressure. A single complete oscillation of pressure comprises a cycle; frequency is usually expressed in cycles per second. Frequency is the principal physical determinant of what we hear as pitch (see G.I.). Higher frequency is usually associated with higher pitch; thus, the more rapidly the vocal folds vibrate, the higher the pitch of the resulting sound.

The term *intensity* is frequently used in a sense roughly synonymous with sound pressure amplitude (i.e., the magnitude of the pressure oscillation). Variations of sound pressure amplitude are closely associated with the perception of *loudness*. The amplitude of excursion of the vocal folds is determined by the force of the outrushing air and is one of the chief determinants of the loudness of vocal sound.

In our daily environment we seldom hear a *pure tone* — one comprised of a single frequency. Instead, we hear complex sounds consisting of many frequencies sounding simultaneously. A complex sound which has a certain pattern of vibration repeated over and over at a given rate is called a *periodic sound*, or tone. An *aperiodic sound* is one which does not have this periodicity of pattern and hence produces no sensation of pitch. We refer to such sounds as *noises*.

A complex periodic tone has a *fundamental* (normally the lowest vibration present) plus many *overtones* (higher pitched frequencies which sound simultaneously). Pitch is determined primarily by the fundamental frequency, but the loudness of a sound is affected by the combined intensities of both the fundamental and its overtones. Tone quality is determined by the overtone structure. It is affected either by changes in the frequency of any of the overtones or by redistribution of the amount of intensity of these frequencies.

The transmission system: Resonation

In addition to the complex vibratory patterns produced by the vocal folds, other determinants of tone quality are the throat, mouth, and nose — the supraglottal *resonators* (see G.I.). Before the vibrations produced by the vocal folds can be freely transmitted through the air, they must pass through the throat and mouth and sometimes the nose. These passages can be viewed as a kind of resonant transmission system which alters the wave composition of vibrations being transmitted through it by reinforcing some frequencies and dampening others.

Resonators tend to reflect and concentrate sound waves more readily at certain frequencies than at others. Accordingly, in transmitting sound through a system with resonance characteristics, those frequencies in the generated sound which most nearly match the resonant frequencies of the transmission system will receive greater amplification than the other frequencies in the tone complex. Such change in wave composition will be reflected in the tone quality of the sound. Hence the pharyngeal, oral, and nasal passages of the human vocal mechanism continually modify the wave composition of the basic laryngeal tone.

Factors which determine the resonance characteristics of the speech mechanism include the size, shape, and texture of the resonating cavities. To these factors must be added the relationship of the size of the apertures — the size of the posterior opening into the mouth and nose in relation to the size of the nostrils or in relation to anterior mouth opening, size, and shape. Moreover, when we consider the great flexibility of the tongue, we can understand what an important part this structure has in continually changing the resonating characteristics of a human voice.

In addition to the obvious ability of the lips, jaw, and tongue to modify the anterior mouth opening, the relationship of the velum, tonsil and adenoid tissue, tongue, and pharyngeal walls to the posterior dimensions and opening of the mouth are also important in determining resonance characteristics. Any change in the normal relationship of all these structures will result in amplifying different overtones, and hence will change the tone quality. We can understand the possible effect on our speech of enlarged tonsils and adenoids, swollen velum, tongue, or lips when we consider the relationship of size, shape, and texture to tone quality.

Speaking in terms of vocal texture, we can also begin to appreciate the vocal effects of excessive tension. Not only does excessive tension of the vocal folds themselves affect the laryngeal tone produced, but tension in the walls of the throat and mouth also plays a part in modifying the tone as it is transmitted through these cavities.

Vowels and Consonants

The information presented in the preceding discussion provides a further means of understanding the vowel and consonant sounds of our language – in terms of resonance and periodicity. Differences between the vowel sounds are for the most part solely changes in resonance, brought about chiefly by different tongue placements and mouth and jaw openings. By such oral modifications, we change the amounts of intensity of the various overtones so that the listener reacts phonemically to the resonance changes – he perceives and identifies different vowel sounds as a result of different resonance conditions. Thus, we come to view vowels acoustically as *resonance phenomena*.

The vocal folds which produce the periodic modulation of the air stream associated with vocal tones are not, however, the sole source of speech sounds. Transient pulses capable of being perceived by the human ear can be generated in the vocal tract by momentarily stopping and suddenly releasing the air stream. We have already classified the sounds thus produced as *stops* (see Chapter 2). Air within the vocal tract may also be set into vibration as a result of the turbulence created by narrowing the vocal tract at some point and forcing air through the resulting narrow aperture. These various parts of the vocal tract which momentarily constrict or obstruct the breath stream serve as *noise* sources. The speech sounds resulting from such constriction or obstruction are discussed in Chapters 2 and 5 under the classification of *consonant sounds*.

All of our vowel sounds are relatively periodic and hence are *tonal* phenomena. The voiceless consonants [p, t, k, f, θ, s, ʃ, tʃ, h] are *aperiodic noises*. The voiced consonants, however, have both periodic (vocal fold tone) and aperiodic (vocal tract constriction) components.

BIBLIOGRAPHY

Aiken, Janet R. *Why English Sounds Change*. New York: The Ronald Press Co., 1929.

————. *English Present and Past.* New York: The Ronald Press Co., 1930.

Albright, Robert William. *The International Phonetic Alphabet: Its Backgrounds and Development*, Publication Seven, Indiana University Research Center in Anthropology, Folklore, and Linguistics. *International Journal of American Linguistics*, XXIV, No. l, pt. 3 (January 1958).

Bloomfield, Leonard. *Language*. New York: Henry Holt & Co., Inc., 1933.

Bronstein, Arthur J. *The Pronunciation of American English: An Introduction to Phonetics*. New York: Appleton-Century-Crofts, Inc., 1960.

Curtis, James F. "Disorders of Voice." In Wendell Johnson et al. (eds.), *Speech Handicapped School Children*, rev. ed. New York: Harper & Brothers, 1956.

Curtis, James F. and James C. Hardy. "A Phonetic Study of Misarticulation of r," *Journal of Speech and Hearing Research*, II (1959), 244-257.

Emsley, Bert, Charles K. Thomas, and Claude Sifritt. "Phonetics and Pronunciation." In Karl R. Wallace et al. (eds.), *A History of Speech Education in America*. New York: Appleton-Century-Crofts, Inc., 1954.

Francis, W. Nelson. *The Structure of American English*. New York: The Ronald Press Company, 1958.

Gleason, H. A., Jr. *An Introduction to Descriptive Linguistics*, rev. ed. New York: Henry Holt & Co., Inc., 1961.

Heffner, Roe-Merrill. *General Phonetics*. Madison: University of Wisconsin Press, 1950.

Hockett, Charles F. *A Course in Modern Linguistics*. New York: The Macmillan Company, 1958.

Hubbell, Allan F. *The Pronunciation of English in New York City*. New York: King's Crown Press, 1950.

Irwin, Ray. "A Problem of Assimilation," *Quarterly Journal of Speech*, XLVI (1960), 302-303.

Jones, Daniel. *An Outline of English Phonetics*, 3rd ed. Cambridge, England: W. Heffer & Sons, Ltd., 1932.

————. *The Pronunciation of English*, 4th ed., rev. & enl. Cambridge, England: Cambridge University Press, 1956.

Kantner, Claude E. and Robert West. *Phonetics*, rev. ed. New York: Harper & Brothers, 1960.

Kenyon, John Samuel. *American Pronunciation*, 10th ed. Ann Arbor, Michigan: George Wahr, 1950.

Krapp, George Philip. *The English Language in America*. New York: F. Ungar Publishing Company, 1960.

————. *The Pronunciation of Standard English in America*. New York: Oxford University Press, Inc., 1919.

Kurath, Hans. *American Pronunciation*. Oxford: The Clarendon Press, 1928.

————. *A Word Geography of the Eastern United States*. Ann Arbor: The University of Michigan Press, 1949.

———— and Raven I. McDavid, Jr. *The Pronunciation of English in the Atlantic States*. Ann Arbor: The University of Michigan Press, 1961.

———— et al. *Handbook of the Linguistic Geography of New England*. Providence, R. I.: Brown University, 1939.

Ladefoged, Peter, M. H. Draper, and D. Whitteridge. "Syllable and Stress," *Miscellanea Phonetica III*. London: International Phonetic Association, (1958), pp. 1-14.

Lloyd, Donald. "Reading American English Sound Patterns" (Unpublished paper read before the Chicago Area Reading Association, May 1961).

———— and Harry R. Warfel. *American English in Its Cultural Setting*. New York: Alfred A. Knopf, Inc., 1956.

Mencken, H. L. *The American Language*, Supplement II. New York: Alfred A. Knopf, Inc., 1948.

Miller, George A. *Language and Communication*. New York: McGraw-Hill Book Co., 1951.

Orbeck, Anders. *Early New England Pronunciation*. Ann Arbor: George Wahr, 1927.

Pike, Kenneth L. *The Intonation of American English*. Ann Arbor: The University of Michigan Press, 1945.

The Principles of the International Phonetic Association. London: NP, 1949.

Pyles, Thomas. *Words and Ways of American English*. New York: Random House, Inc., 1952.

Stetson, Raymond H. *Motor Phonetics: A Study of Speech Movements in Action*, 2nd ed. Amsterdam: North Holland Publishing Co., 1951.

Sweet, Henry. *A History of English Sounds*. London: Trubner and Co., 1874.

Thomas, Charles Kenneth. *An Introduction to the Phonetics of American English*, 2nd ed. New York: The Ronald Press Co., 1958.

Trager, George L. and Henry Lee Smith, Jr. *An Outline of English Structure*, Studies in Linguistics, Occasional Papers No. 3. Norman, Oklahoma: Battenburg Press, 1951.

Travis, Lee Edward (ed.). *Handbook of Speech Pathology*. New York: Appleton-Century-Crofts, Inc., 1957.

Van Riper, Charles. *Speech Correction: Principles and Methods*, 3rd ed. Englewood Cliffs, N.J.: Prentice-Hall, Inc., 1954.

Wise, Claude Merton. *Applied Phonetics*. Englewood Cliffs, N.J.: Prentice-Hall, Inc., 1957.

Pronouncing and Dialect Dictionaries

Bender, James F. (comp.). *NBC Handbook of Pronunciation*, 2nd ed. with suppl. New York: Thomas Y. Crowell Company, 1955.

Greet, W. Cabell. *World Words*, 2nd ed., rev. and enl. New York: Columbia University Press, 1948.

Jones, Daniel. *Everyman's English Pronouncing Dictionary*, 11th ed. New York: E. P. Dutton & Co., Inc., 1956.

Kenyon, John S. and Thomas A. Knott. *A Pronouncing Dictionary of American English*, 2nd ed. Springfield, Massachusetts: G. & C. Merriam Co., 1949.

Wentworth, Harold. *American Dialect Dictionary*. New York: Thomas Y. Crowell Company, 1944.

General Dictionaries

The American College Dictionary. New York: Random House, Inc.

A Dictionary of American English on Historical Principles, 4 vol. Chicago: University of Chicago Press.

Funk & Wagnalls New Practical Standard Dictionary of the English Language. New York: Funk & Wagnalls Company.

Funk & Wagnalls Standard Dictionary of the English Language: International Edition. New York: Funk & Wagnalls Company.

New College Standard Dictionary. New York: Funk & Wagnalls Company.

Thorndike-Barnhart Comprehensive Desk Dictionary. New York: Doubleday & Company, Inc.

Webster's New Collegiate Dictionary. Springfield, Massachusetts: G. & C. Merriam Co.

Webster's Seventh New Collegiate Dictionary. Springfield, Massachusetts: G. & C. Merriam Co.

Webster's New World Dictionary of the American Language: College Edition. New York: The World Publishing Company.

Webster's Third New International Dictionary of the English Language, Unabridged. Springfield, Massachusetts: G. & C. Merriam Co.

GLOSSARIAL INDEX

The page numbers refer to the page on which the term is defined, described, or explained. Definitions are included in this index only for those terms not clarified in the text discussion.

on-glide 25 *the "approach phase" of a sound (For each speech sound the articulators momentarily assume a definite position. The movement of the articulators between these positions, when accompanied by an uninterrupted flow of sound, results in transitional sounds, or glides. The "approach phase" of such transitional sounds is called the on-glide; the transition away from the speech sound is the off-glide.)*

oralpharyngeal tract 36 *the part of the speech pathway comprised of the mouth and throat*

orthography 3 *"grammar treating of letters and spelling" (Webster, p. 593)*

overtones 161

palate, hard 23
palate, soft 23
palatal glide 35
palato-alveolar 72
partial (incomplete) assimilation 145
periodic sound 161
pharynx 22, 159
phonemes 1
  pitch 151
  segmental *(see segmental phonemes)*
  suprasegmental *(see suprasegmental phonemes)*
phonemic transcription 26
phonetics 1, 53
phrasal stress 137
pitch 6, 160 *highness or lowness of a tone on the musical scale*
pitch phonemes 151
plosive 25
polsysyllabic 8
port, nasal (velopharyngeal) *(see nasal port)*
postvocalic 8
postvocalic *r* 102
prescriptive phonetics 53
prevocalic 8
primary stress 53, 136
progressive assimilation 146
pronunciation standards 6
protrusion lisp 32
pure tone 160
pure vowel 48 *vowel made with no noticeable movement of the articulators during its production (as contrasted with the movement necessary to produce a diphthong)*

quality (of vocal tone) 150 *". . . the vocal color; the characteristic by which we distinguish between two voices uttering the same vowel at the same pitch, or between two different vowels uttered by the same voice at the same pitch" (West, Ansberry and Carr, pp. 623-624)*

r-coloring 62, 103
[r], postvocalic 102
[r], retroflex 35
[r], vocalic (vowelized) 59
reciprocal assimilation 149
regressive assimilation 144
resonance phenomena 162
resonant frequencies 161
resonators (of vocal mechanism) 161 *air-filled cavities which modify the quality of a laryngeal tone passing through them*
respiration 158
retracting diphthong 100
retroflex *r* 35
reversed epsilon 62

schwa 60
  hooked 62
secondary stress 53, 136
segmental phonemes 151 *consonant and vowel phonemes*
semantics 1 *the science of meanings*
semivowel 78, 102
separability 74
soft palate 23
sound pressure amplitude 160
Southern speech region 6
speech regions 6
square brackets 9
stop 25
stress 53, 60
  four-degree system (primary, secondary, tertiary, weak) 136
  phrasal 137
  syllabic 137
stress, symbol for 53
subglottal 160 *below the glottis*
supra-glottal 161 *above the glottis*
suprasegmental elements 151 *stress, pitch, and juncture elements (Juncture — the mode of transition from one speech-segment to another — is not discussed in this text.)*
syllabic 66 *speech sound which by itself makes a syllable or subordinates to itself the other sounds in a syllable*
syllabic consonant 66
syllabic mark 66
syllabic stress 137
syllable 8
symbol for:
  aspiration 25